NO LONGER
OWNED BY
HOLDREGE AREA PUBLIC LIBRARY

HOLDREGE AREA PUBLIC LIBRARY
604 EAST AVENUE
HOLDREGE, NE 68949

Testimonials

"I was interviewed by a local author, Sandra Hilsabeck, and I would like to express my delight in being a grandma. Although this development was unexpected, unplanned, and a surprise, it is so clear that my new grandbaby is surely a part of God's divine plan. From the womb through the present, this baby is fulfilling his God-given purpose to the world and his loving family. About this book, I told Sandra, 'This is beautiful! I literally hung on every word of your introduction, and I *know* that many will be blessed by your words of wisdom captured in a special way."

—Angela Pillow, Public Relations Ambassador
and Administrative Associate for City Impact, Lincoln, NE

"*Ready or Not: 10 Reasons to Love Your Baby* by Sandra Hilsabeck-Hastings beautifully confirms what we all probably know in our hearts; namely, that God's mission for us as human beings is to support life and nurture it, no matter the circumstances or difficulties in which we find ourselves. It is a very thoughtful treatment of a controversial subject that reaffirms the power of God to heal and strengthen us as we face difficult choices in our lives. A job well done and a book well worth the reading."

—Carmen Hill Grant, PhD,
Retired Clinical Psychologist and Psychotherapist
Lincoln, NE

"Sandra Hilsabeck's *Ready or Not: 10 Reasons to Love Your Baby* connects two great God-glorifying choices: not to abort a baby and adoption. Being the personal recipient of both choices, I'm excited for you to be reminded in this book that Jesus Christ paid a huge price for every life, and every life is precious to Him."

—Ron Brown
Associate Head Coach and Wide Receivers Coach
at Liberty University at Lynchburg, VA

READY OR NOT

10 Reasons to Love Your Baby

[signature] John 15:9-12

SANDRA HILSABECK

WESTBOW
PRESS
A DIVISION OF THOMAS NELSON
& ZONDERVAN

Copyright © 2015 Sandra Hilsabeck.

All rights reserved. No part of this book may be used or reproduced by any means, graphic, electronic, or mechanical, including photocopying, recording, taping or by any information storage retrieval system without the written permission of the publisher except in the case of brief quotations embodied in critical articles and reviews.

Stories in this book may be copied for teaching purposes. Copying portions larger than one story need to be approved by the author.

Unless otherwise noted, all Scripture quotations are taken from the *Holy Bible, New International Version* ®, copyright © 1973, 1978, 1984 by International Bible Society from the 1990 Women's Devotional Bible and 1995 Women's Devotional Bible 2. Used by permission of Zondervan Publishing House. All rights reserved.

Some Scripture quotations are taken from *The Message*, copyright © by Eugene H. Peterson 1993, 1994, 1995, 1996, 2000, 2001, 2002. Used by permission of NavPress Publishing Group. All rights reserved.

Some Scripture quotations are taken from *The Living Bible,* copyright © 1971 by Tyndale House Publishers, Wheaton, Illinois 60187. All rights reserved.

Permission given for all quotes, poems, and hymn.

WestBow Press books may be ordered through booksellers or by contacting:

WestBow Press
A Division of Thomas Nelson & Zondervan
1663 Liberty Drive
Bloomington, IN 47403
www.westbowpress.com
1 (866) 928-1240

Because of the dynamic nature of the Internet, any web addresses or links contained in this book may have changed since publication and may no longer be valid. The views expressed in this work are solely those of the author and do not necessarily reflect the views of the publisher, and the publisher hereby disclaims any responsibility for them.

Any people depicted in stock imagery provided by Thinkstock are models, and such images are being used for illustrative purposes only. Certain stock imagery © Thinkstock.

ISBN: 978-1-4908-7670-2 (sc)
ISBN: 978-1-4908-7671-9 (hc)
ISBN: 978-1-4908-7669-6 (e)

Library of Congress Control Number: 2015905998

Print information available on the last page.

WestBow Press rev. date: 06/03/2015

Disclaimer

A number of the stories use pseudonyms to protect the persons telling their stories, and members of their families.

All stories are real-life happenings and have been approved by the people interviewed.

This book may be ordered through WestBow Press, Barnes & Noble, or Amazon and Google, or by contacting the author.

Contents

Preface xi
Acknowledgments xix
Introduction xxi

1. **Your Child Might Grow to Serve Mankind** 1
   (1) The Word Adopt Meant Love - Brown 3
   (2) Through Struggles, Love Prevails - Hastings 10
   (3) Action of Love by One Adopted - Lentfer 18
   (4) She Found Love at Every Address - Sim 22

2. **Children Are an Unbelievable Blessing** 31
   (5) Finding Love after the Years - Philson 33
   (6) Love at First Sight - Jenkins 39
   (7) Comfortable in a Loving Home - Stark 44
   (8) Two Ways to Get Kids and Love Them Both - D. Tonack 55

3. **God Prepares Families for Children** 59
   (9) Unselfish Behavior Shows Love - Holmberg 61
   (10) God Prepared the Way for Love - Eley 66
   (11) The Girls Needed Her, and Her Purpose Was to
        Love - Pillow 71
   (12) The Child They Were Supposed to Love - Lennox 74

4. Adoptions Offer Parents Choices 79
(13) Open Adoption Shows Love and Trust - Vagts 81
(14) Love Is the Reward of a Life Decision - White 90
(15) Ready to Love a Child - Lehr 94

5. Agencies Choose Adoptive Parents Carefully 99
(16) God Works for the Good of Those Who Love Him - Michener 101
(17) You Are My Real Mom, and I Love You - Haun 108

6. Children Love Parents Who Adopt Them 113
(18) My Family History Is Love - Budka 115
(19) Discipline Is a Gift of Love - Pieper 119
(20) Love Kept Her from Anger and Blame - Fredstrom 124
(21) One Born to Large Family Finds Love in Small One - T. Tonack 130
(22) I Am Loved, and Life Is Full - Lau 133

7. Parents Who Adopt Show Tremendous Love to Children 137
(23) Mission of Love Began on Mission Trip - LaTorre 139
(24) Love Heals, Understanding Gives Worth - McPherson 142
(25) Love Provided to Blended Family - Ragatz 148
(26) Love Perseveres - Yoder 152
(27) The Great Size of an Adoptive Mother's Love - Kilian 157

8. Love from Temporary, Foster, and Guardian Parents ... 165
(28) Love Them as If They Were Our Own - Johnson 167
(29) Showing Great Love - Kennedy 170
(30) Love Returned in Abundance - Geist 175

9. Responsible Choices Offer Life 181
(31) One Human Saved by Love - Bellus 183
(32) Don't Hurt the Grandbaby I Love - Waters 186

(33) Three Ladies Taught About Love - Hout 189
(34) Pregnancy Takes Her to Loving Arms - Traci 196
(35) God's Love and Mercy - Percourt 201

10. Amazing Human Love 207
(36) Mixed Adoptions Done with Love - Jacobson 209
(37) Adopting Love Affects Triad - Ishler 215
(38) A Father's Love - Nicklas 219
(39) Adopted Because of Love for Others - Holen 225

Afterword 231
Hymn by Thomas Jackson "We Are Called to Be God's
    People" 235
Sources 237

Preface

My Story of Parental Love

It was early in the 1960s. I, your author, was raised on a farm, went to one-room elementary schools, and attended high school in town. I was very naïve, stupid, you might say. That was why I got pregnant at age fifteen. I feel that I must tell my story in order to help you understand why I truly believe that God controls even the time that fertilization of an egg occurs.

As a sixteen-year-old, I was saved from doing something disastrous to myself and my baby. I could not tell my parents I was pregnant. I didn't want to hurt them. My mother and I had been going together to see the doctor to find out what was wrong with me. One day my mother could not come with me, so I went alone. I was shocked to hear what the doctor had to say. He told me I was pregnant. I didn't believe him. I was skinny, immature, and had not yet settled into regular periods. Yet I was nauseated most of the time and had started to gain weight. This was strange because I wasn't eating more than normal, and I was riding my bicycle to work. I tried to think about where I could run the car off a cliff, but Nebraska is a pretty flat state.

Since then, I and the father of that baby have been married to other spouses and have had children with them, but to this day, fifty-some years later, we cannot understand what happened. We had experimented together a couple of times, but we hadn't felt that we had even completed the act. I'd felt that I was still a virgin. I had been infatuated with him and wanted to please him. The fact that I got pregnant so easily led me to understand that God wanted this baby to be born. God was in control and had allowed this pregnancy to happen. He had made me very fertile, which I learned later when I decided to have more children. I knew that I would have a baby within a year after going off the contraceptive.

I was already five months pregnant when I found out. Abortion was not an option, and it was illegal anyway. I had no idea how an abortion was done or where to get one. I didn't understand it at the time, but I became a better person after having my daughter when I was sixteen years old. Maybe this was one of the reasons God allowed this pregnancy to occur. Many changes came about for me, and I learned and matured rapidly. I became a better daughter, friend, sister, and person.

"Consider it pure joy, my brothers, whenever you face trials of many kinds, because you know that the testing of your faith develops perseverance. Perseverance must finish its work so that you may be mature and complete, not lacking anything" (James 1:2–4). I am sure you realize that I did not consider my becoming a pregnant teenager something to be joyous about. But God knew what would happen to me in this circumstance. "'For I know the plans I have for you,' declares the LORD, 'plans to prosper you and not to harm you, plans to give you hope and a future. Then you will call upon me and come and pray to me, and I will listen to you. You will seek me and find me when you seek me with all your heart'" (Jeremiah 29:11–13). Do you suppose God knew that fifty years later I would be telling my story to help others? I do. I have seen Him in action too many times not to believe it, and I have learned to seek Him with all my heart.

I learned that my family loved me anyway. It was my aunt who took me out to our farm and told my parents. At the time, I was living with her and my uncle in town so I could take care of my 4-H calf at the county fair and work at the public swimming pool. My dad was so mad that he left for the barn, and I could tell how much I had hurt my mother. I would never have purposely done that to them. Another aunt helped my mom understand that I wasn't out trying to hurt them or shame them. My boyfriend was a star athlete in multiple sports, and I was young and was swept away by him. No one had told me not to experiment. No one had expected sexual experimentation at such a young age. Remember, it was middle America, farm country, and the year 1961. My boyfriend told me years later that he felt my parents responded to this crisis with love. My younger sister heard us all crying in the kitchen, and she told me she learned from my experience.

The public judged me. I was expelled from school. I could take correspondence courses from the university, which I immediately did. I wanted to graduate with my class. Never again was I allowed to be in the Pep Club or other school activities. This humbled me. My friends in my supper club (a club that met for dinner before Friday night games) told me to keep coming to our club. They even let me bring my beautiful little girl sometimes. These friends had known me before; they knew my character and seemed to understand the situation. I lost my job; it wouldn't have been right for me to teach swimming lessons, because I wasn't a good role model anymore. In the year of our fiftieth class reunion, two class members mentioned to me that they wished they had stood up to the authorities and told them the penalty was too harsh. They blessed me with these comments. My close friends and family always stood by me.

The aunt who consulted with my mom showed me that Christians accept those who have sinned. She invited me to play the piano in her Sunday school class and help her teach. This was my first experience of forgiveness outside of my parents. An aunt from the other side of the family welcomed me into her arms, and another said she would be willing to raise my daughter with her four little boys. My entire family welcomed my little girl, and she became the delight of our farm home. My grandparents treated me with love and forgiveness. Grandma Bessie sat me down on her couch one day and told me it would be all right. She said there would be better days. I was so embarrassed that I didn't ask any questions. Now I wish I could talk to her today. I look forward to the day she greets me in heaven.

When the time came for my daughter to be born, my mother took me to the hospital, stopping by Grandma's house as we went, because she was having one of her family reunions. I was in labor for twelve hours and ended up having a caesarean section. Later, I experienced a near-death situation, as I had toxemia and rolled out of bed, breaking open many of a long row of stitches. There were no bikini cuts at that time.

When I finally woke up several days later, there was my mother. She was sitting in the chair in my room, holding this beautiful baby. The baby's head was white and smooth, and her face wasn't wrinkly like some newborns. Caesarean babies don't have the trauma of the birth canal. The first words my mother said to me were, "Isn't she precious?" I knew the shame I had brought my mother, though I didn't know about the agony she'd felt in almost losing me. But on that day, she greeted me with her love for my baby. I am shedding tears as I write this. It was unconditional love, like the love God gives us. I had done nothing to deserve it, but I received it anyway.

Without my parents, I would not have been able to care for my daughter and continue my education. My mother and father sacrificed many days and nights to help me parent so that I could continue my life. I went back to school for my senior year and then on to college on a scholarship. My daughter was four years old when I chose to marry and move 160 miles away from home. My mother knew that I would be raising my daughter eventually, but when I took her from that farm home, my mother was very lonely. This little girl was something special and had been a companion for her. I had caused my mother to experience the loss of a small child leaving home, which can be an even greater loss than the empty nest we experience when adult children leave. What I did affected so many others.

My little girl is now the mother of four children, whom I would never have known had someone told me they could solve my problem with an abortion. I would never have had a daughter, as I later had two sons. Now my husband and I have fourteen grandchildren, and we communicate with, see, and travel with all of them. I admire, enjoy, and treasure this daughter. She planned a recent vacation for us and her two daughters. It was a grand trip to Paris and Lyon, France. God has blessed us.

My daughter's biological father and I are friends. We were in love and intended to marry. I understand that he was young, and he made the choice to obey his parents when he was sent away after they found out I was pregnant. They realized that he was too young and ill prepared to accept the responsibility of a wife and child. We are both thankful that my parents decided to love us and help me. He has always known his daughter, has seen her on occasion, and has met her family. I was very impressed with his character when he chose not to interfere with my husband and me while raising her. He also allowed my husband to adopt his daughter. He loved his little girl and was definitely sad that he was not able to raise her as his own.

At times I feared there would never be a man who would want to accept a child and a wife. I was surprised when five men asked me to marry them. I thought this quite unusual because after dating for some time, I always told them I had a little girl at home. This child would come with me when I married—a two-for-one situation. Because of my mother's love toward me, I knew I needed to think of my daughter's needs instead of just my own.

My college beau was a nice young man, but he had been raised in a military family and wanted me to move far away from home. I wanted to keep my daughter close to her grandparents, who had helped me so much. A friend I dated was a wonderful person, but we didn't date long enough for me to fall in love with him. He offered marriage and support to my daughter and me, but I never felt that a sufficient reason to marry. A wonderful person at college was graduating and moving away when he asked me to join him. In those days, that meant, "Let's get married." We did not know any couple that was "living together" without marriage. I was just a sophomore in college, attending on the scholarship I'd earned for being seventh in my graduating class. I wanted to finish and become an interpreter with a Spanish degree. Then I could support my daughter and myself.

Before my daughter's father came back to town and asked me to marry him, I had fallen in love with a man who was graduating from college. He wanted my daughter as part of his family, and he had an extended family that I loved and enjoyed being around. His two younger brothers were like little brothers to me. He wanted to get married immediately. I felt that this was the choice I should make for my daughter and myself. She was already four years old.

These verses from the Bible lead me to believe that God knows the soul of a baby even before conception. "Long before he laid down earth's foundations, he had us in mind, had settled on us as the focus of his love, to be made whole and holy by his love. Long, long ago he decided to adopt us into his family through Jesus Christ" (Ephesians 1:4–5 MSG). "You created my inmost being; you knit me together in my mother's womb. I praise you because I am fearfully and wonderfully made; your works are wonderful, I know that full well. My frame was not hidden from you when I was made in the secret place. When I was woven together in the depths of the earth, your eyes saw my unformed body. All the days ordained for me were written in your book before one of them came to be" (Psalm 139:13–16).

Once I had an opportunity to stop an abortion when a young mother came to me. I didn't even try to change her mind, and it has concerned me ever since. I might have been able to save a life. It is not very often that we are given that opportunity. You will see a story in this book where my niece saved a baby. Thank goodness that my sins are forgiven. God sees all sins alike. "He is as quick to show mercy to the man who asks forgiveness for lying as he is to the man who seeks forgiveness for abortion," says the book entitled *Fatherhood Aborted* by Guy Condon and David Hazard.

I learned that my sin affects not only me but many others surrounding me. I find consolation in these Scriptures.

> As for you, you were dead in your transgressions and sins, in which you used to live when you followed the ways of this world and of the ruler of the kingdom of the air, the spirit who is now at work in those who are disobedient. All of us also lived among them at one time, gratifying the cravings of our sinful nature and following its desires and thoughts. Like the rest, we were by nature objects of wrath. But because of his great love for us, God, who is rich in mercy, made us alive with Christ even when we were dead in transgressions—it is by grace you have been saved. (Ephesians 2:1–5)

"And we know that in all things God works for the good of those who love him" (Romans 8:28).

Nothing that has happened to us should be wasted. May my telling this story be a blessing to you.

Turning to You

In the *Star Tribune* (Minneapolis), Gail Rosenblum wrote, "Women never forgot babies they surrendered in bygone era. Far from being promiscuous, as they were labeled, some got pregnant the first time they had sex or were admittedly clueless about birth control, reproduction or how a baby is born."

If you find yourself pregnant, look for a crisis pregnancy center where there is help for you and your baby. They will provide help if you keep your baby, or they will guide you to local adoption services where various options of adoption are available to you.

Pat McCarthy, director of a crisis pregnancy center, says, "Sex is like a fire in a fireplace. If left there, it does the job it is supposed to do. It is hot, burns the appropriate wood, and heats the room. All enjoy it. Likewise, sex inside of marriage does what it is supposed to do. It solidifies the marriage, makes the husband and wife closer in a unique relationship, and provides for children. However, if it is allowed where it doesn't belong, it is like fire out of the fireplace and creates all kinds of troubles."

Prayer

Thank You, Lord, for blessing me with children and grandchildren. I know the lost feeling many women feel when they are pregnant and not ready to marry. Please be with them and guide them with Your wisdom. Lord, help us remember these words: "Then he [Jesus] said to them, 'Whoever welcomes this little child in my name welcomes me; and whoever welcomes me welcomes the one who sent me. For he who is least among you all—he is the greatest'" (Luke 9:48). Amen.

Acknowledgments

I would like to acknowledge my storytellers for meeting with me and working with me until their stories were written in a way that would honor their families. Thank you to all who have prayed for God's will to be done during the writing, publishing, and distribution of this book. I am thankful for all the encouragement and timely advice provided by my husband, Bryce, my sister Linoma Wingate, and many friends, especially Jerilyn Delzell.

Also, God has played the most important part in the making of this book. He has given me the exact verses I needed when I needed them as I studied His Word. He introduced me to these wonderful people who have adopted or cared for children, and who have opened their hearts and agreed to tell their stories.

Introduction

You will notice that the word *love* is in every title of this book. As I interviewed the people who had been adopted, the parents who had adopted children, and workers in the field of adoptions, I was very impressed with the care and love they expressed. In every instance of a parent placing a child for adoption, it took more love to release the child to others than it would have taken to keep the child. In this book, *Ready or Not: 10 Reasons to Love Your Baby*, you will see how God works in the lives of us humans. Only God could bring some of these families together. I believe there are no coincidences and that God is with us every step of our way.

Jesus was adopted by His earthly father, Joseph. If you have seen the film *Nativity Story*, you can easily believe that Joseph was not convinced that he should marry Mary when he found out she was pregnant. It took an angel to change his mind. "But after he had considered this, an angel of the Lord appeared to him in a dream and said, 'Joseph son of David, do not be afraid to take Mary home as your wife, because what is conceived in her is from the Holy Spirit. She will give birth to a son, and you are to give him the name Jesus, because he will save his people from their sins'" (Matthew 1:20–21).

We can believe that there were no papers filed, but Joseph helped Mary protect and raise Jesus, following the directions given by God through the angel Gabriel and the Holy Spirit. God had chosen them to be the earthly parents of His Son. He knew what a stretch that assignment was for them. God brought people to them in the early days—everyday people whose lives were transformed—to confirm Jesus' deity. In addition to shepherds and wise men, there were Simeon and Anna, people whom God directed to come to the temple to tell Mary and Joseph that they had been waiting for Jesus, God's Son.

We are also adopted by God as heirs with Christ. "His unchanging plan has always been to adopt us into his own family by sending Jesus Christ to die for us. And he did this because he wanted to!" (Ephesians 1:5 LB). We are heirs, according to this next verse: "He saved us through the washing of rebirth and renewal by the Holy Spirit, whom he poured out on us generously through Jesus Christ our Savior, so that having been justified by his grace, we might become heirs having the hope of eternal life" (Titus 3:5b–7).

Many women pleaded for abortion to become legal so we wouldn't have back-alley clinics that were dirty and unsafe. But we still have them. And money-hungry doctors that prey on our most innocent are being tried in the courts today. The stories in *Ready or Not: 10 Reasons to Love Your Baby* show love being given to normal children with all their faculties, as well as to those who have disease and mental struggles. We have these great words from Paul, a disciple of Christ: "Do nothing out of selfish ambition or vain conceit, but in humility consider others better than yourselves. Each of you should look not only to your own interests, but also to the interests of others" (Philippians 2:3–4). "Do not murder ... Love your neighbor as yourself" (Romans 13:9b, d).

Two of the adopting families in this book felt that "someone was missing" before they adopted. Love is found in foster, adoptive, and guardian homes the same as it is in homes where children are born to the parents. "All babies can be loved by someone," says Ron Brown, whose adoption was a genuine miracle.

For the pregnant mother (or it could be the father) who is not ready to marry and raise the child they've conceived within a family, there are three obvious options used today:

1. Eliminate the baby.
2. Raise the baby alone.
3. Place the baby for adoption.

For the mother or father who does not have tremendous support from family or friends, placing your child for adoption can be a gift from God. God may already have prepared a family that is ready to raise this wonderful miracle of yours. As you read this book, you will discover the joy and love a child receives when given the chance to be raised in a stable family with a mom and dad. Sue Anne Philson said this about her adoption: "What one family considered to be a mistake and a terrible thing, God used to bring joy and happiness to another family."

Purpose for *Ready or Not, 10 Reasons to Love Your Baby*

My purpose, with love for you,
is aptly stated by the apostle Paul: "My purpose is that
they [you] may be encouraged in heart and united in *love*,
so that they [you] may have the full riches
of complete understanding,
in order that they [you] may know
the mystery of God, namely,
Christ, in whom are hidden all the treasures of wisdom and
knowledge.
I tell you this so that no one may deceive you
by fine-sounding arguments.
For though I am absent from you in body,
I am present with you in spirit
and delight to see how orderly you are
and how firm your faith in Christ is"

(Colossians 2:2–5, emphasis added).

God Created the Amazing Human Being

Then there is man, the zenith of God's creative genius. God made him with eyes to behold the beauty of nature, ears to hear its lovely sounds, nostrils to enjoy its pleasant aromas, taste buds to relish its infinite variety of eatable delights, a sense of touch to help communicate love to someone precious to him, and a mind to comprehend the meaning of it all, to name just a few evidences of God's goodness. He affords us no end of good things; the warmth of sunlight, the joy of loving family and friends, the satisfaction of productive labor, the exhilaration of physical exercise and recreation, the refreshment of a good night's sleep, provision for our daily needs, and so many others that enrich our lives. These blessings turn our minds to Him in adoration and gratitude. (Richard L. Strauss, *The Joy of Knowing God*)

Reason 1

Your Child Might Grow to Serve Mankind

1

The Word *Adopt* Meant Love

Ron Brown

The Foundling in New York City still exists in the Bronx. A young man from India studying engineering met a young African-American lady from Tennessee. The lady, Marie Price, was twenty-four years old when she called to tell the young man from India that she thought she was pregnant with his child. She never heard back from him, and sure enough, a healthy baby boy was born eight months later. Left alone with many music studies ahead of her, Marie contacted The Foundling and asked if they would take her baby. The adoptions arranged at the orphanage closed further communication between child and parents, and Marie never saw her baby again.

There was a couple named Arthur and Pearl Brown, who were of modest means and worked on Martha's Vineyard, Massachusetts. They had never been able to have children, but they had a lot of love to give. Because they had little money, were both older than forty, and had never finished high school, they felt they would always be childless. One of Mr. Brown's jobs was as a groundskeeper, and Pearl was a cook and a maid. As they worked one day, a wealthy vacationer visited with them. The vacationer mentioned that she was chairman of the board for a New York City orphanage. She saw the many children who had very little chance of being adopted and found it interesting this couple would love to have a family.

Helen Chindlund had a mind to act. No, she was told, there are no out-of-state adoptions being allowed. Helen continued working for the Browns' case and finally broke through all the red tape. She brought the Browns to The Foundling in New York City to search for a baby. They chose little Ron and took him home.

Ron has a different way of looking at this event. He says they took him home and called him their son. You can almost see a tear in this very accomplished man's eyes when he says this phrase. "They called me their son," he says, almost like it was an impossible feat. He is very moved that they could take a child of two years old and act like he was born to them.

Not only did Ron now have parents, but they also adopted a girl who was born to parents who were only fourteen and sixteen years old. This chosen sister completed his family. Now he would be raised with love and devotion. He explains the love like this: "My sister and I were put on our parents' laps every night and had the *Bible for Tots* read to us." Not only did Pearl and Arthur hold their two children, but they also read to the children and put them to bed with love. Arthur and Pearl also told their children that God loved them with all His heart.

Ron remembers Arthur and Pearl telling them, "We are your parents, and we love you. We adopted you, and we love you as our own. You were not born to us; you are adopted. But that doesn't make any difference in our love." This convinced Ron that the word "adopt" had something to do with love—even when he was too young to know what the word meant. He and his sister were ridiculed and pointed out as different by various children and adults as they were growing up; but they always knew that they were enveloped in a special love at home.

You may think that Arthur and Pearl were religious, but they had not trusted Christ as their Savior and Lord. Ron was saved by doing just that at the age of twenty-two, and he proceeded toward seeing both his parents accept Christ. This was a case where the child led the parents. Ron had overcome many obstacles, graduated with an Ivy League degree, and had a contract to play with the Dallas Cowboys as a professional football player. At that time, however, he began to believe that he was too weak to control his life. He knew he needed something more. Establishing a relationship with Christ filled him with the one who had created him. He needed to share that with his parents.

Arthur died just two years after Ron led him to Christ. As Ron tells this great story, you can see his love for his adoptive father, and his happiness in knowing that he will see his father again in heaven. Shortly thereafter, Ron's mother, who initially struggled to believe that Jesus would die for her personally, came to an understanding that He actually did. Just before Pearl had what was thought to be a routine surgical procedure for her heart, she had Ron read Psalm 31:15a to her: "My times are in your hands." This verse had become near and dear to her heart. The next day, after surgery, she died with Ron holding her hand. He had led his mom and dad to the Lord. You can see a yearning for reunion in Ron's face as he tells about this meaningful time of watching his parents leave the world and go to their final resting place.

God has placed a yearning for home in all people. We all understand the joy of being home after a trying day at work, or returning home after a vacation. Ron, as a believing Christian, understands that his eternal home is where God has prepared a place for him and his parents after a short time on earth.

The adopted son led his parents into God's family. Ephesians 1:4–8 explains: "For he [God] chose us in him before the creation of the world to be holy and blameless in his sight. In love he predestined us to be adopted as his sons through Jesus Christ, in accordance with his pleasure and will- to the praise of his glorious grace, which he has freely given us in the One he loves. In him we have redemption through his blood, the forgiveness of sins, in accordance with the riches of God's grace that he lavished on us with all wisdom and understanding."

Ron and his sister were never shielded from the fact that they were adopted. They were never kept from finding their biological parents. Ron's sister was able to find her biological parents, but Ron is still hoping that Marie Price will someday show up on some ancestry website or at his front door. She would be very proud of him, as he stands firm on the Word of the Bible, even when he is threatened by the secular world. His many talents have brought him to the University of Nebraska as a coach. You may have seen him as he administered the prayer at the Penn State stadium for the first football game after Penn State's troubling sexual abuse scandal. The eyes of the nation were on him, and we Nebraskans were never prouder.

Yes, Ron is firm in his belief, and he has led many people into the peace of knowing Jesus Christ as Savior. As he speaks to various groups, he quotes Colossians 3:5–10.

> Put to death, therefore, whatever belongs to your earthly nature: sexual immorality, impurity, lust, evil desires and greed, which is idolatry. Because of these, the wrath of God is coming. You used to walk in these ways, in the life you once lived. But now you must rid yourselves of all such things as these: anger, rage, malice, slander, and filthy language from your lips. Do not lie to each other, since you have taken off your old self with its practices and have put on the new self, which is being renewed in knowledge in the image of its Creator.

Holding to these truths cannot always be easy when coaching a Division I football team in our current culture.

Understanding well that some football players come from backgrounds without parental love, Ron tells of coaching a football game between Kansas State and Nebraska in Tokyo, Japan. Football teams in Japan take only three or four days a year off from practice. This dedication results in playing only four or five games a year and provides a lot of stress for the players. There were sixty thousand people at the Kansas-Nebraska game, but the audience had a misunderstanding. Their biggest cheers were when an extra point kick passed through the goal posts. After the football game, there was a grandiose car show in the stadium, which explained why many of the spectators were there.

Something was missing in the football game in Japan. Football fans in the United States understand that practice is meant to produce good games for a season, and touchdowns provide more points than extra points. The hardworking, intellectual Japanese fail to receive the joy of the game.

Something is missing with us too when trophies and honors are our only goals. Our work and our play need to be worthy as with one mind and one spirit, not separating our lives into a secular part and a sacred part.

Eugene H. Peterson's paraphrase of the Bible, *The Message*, explains very well, in its introduction to Nehemiah, our work and our play as being of one mind and spirit.

> Separating life into distinct categories of "sacred" and "secular" damages, sometimes irreparably, any attempt to live a whole and satisfying life, a coherent life with meaning and purpose, a life lived to the glory of God. Nevertheless, the practice is widespread. But where did all these people come up with the habit of separating themselves and the world around them into these two camps? It surely wasn't from the Bible. The Holy Scriptures, from beginning to end, strenuously resist such a separation. The damage to life is most obvious when the separation is applied to daily work. It is common for us to refer

to the work of pastors, priest, and missionaries as "sacred," and that of lawyers, farmers, and engineers as "secular." It is also wrong. Work, by its very nature, is holy. The biblical story is dominated by people who have jobs in gardening, shepherding, the military, politics, carpentry, tent making, homemaking, fishing, and more.

Ron knows the value of Jeremiah 15:19: "Therefore this is what the LORD says: 'If you repent, I will restore you that you may serve me; if you utter worthy, not worthless, words (in all you do), you will be my spokesman, Let this people turn to you, but you must not turn to them.'"

Love is thicker than blood, in Ron's mind, and he is proof of it. He believes that God has a plan for all babies, and that He knows when each is born and when each is conceived. It is God's sovereign will when a baby is born. Even if that baby is not adopted by an earthly family, any child who has come to faith in Christ becomes a part of God's household. It says in Ephesians 2:18–19, "For through him [Jesus] we both have access to the Father by one Spirit. Consequently, you are no longer foreigners and aliens, but fellow citizens with God's people and members of God's household."

Turning to You

Can you believe that Helen Chindlund was able to accomplish Ron's adoption? A lesser person would have given up after receiving all those "no" answers. God's plans for Ron Brown were bigger than a few rules. It is truly a miracle that Ron had Arthur and Pearl for parents during most of his growing up years. Through his radio show, Fellowship of Christian Athletes, and other ministries, Ron has been able to provide his parents and thousands of others with an understanding of what Jesus did for us on the cross.

This quote gives one man's explanation as to why God provided His only Son to die for us who are sinners: "He wanted so much to manifest His love that He first created the angelic hosts and later the human race so that he might communicate Himself to them, give of Himself for them, and bestow His very best on them for their benefit and blessing" (Richard L. Strauss, *The Joy of Knowing God*).

Prayer

Dear Father in heaven, help us all to be as firm and courageous in our beliefs as Ron Brown. Help us to honor God and love our parents in all situations, in our work and in our play. Amen.

2

Through Struggles, Love Prevails

Steve Hastings

In Steve's own words, he feels that he was adopted twice. He learned at the age of seventeen that he was adopted. This led him to find his birth father. It was exciting, at first, to find Paul David Goff, who welcomed him into his family. Paul said, "Look, you have all these brothers and sisters." As Steve came to know the struggling musician, keyboard player, and singer, he saw the difficult, harder side of life, which he had not known in the family that raised him. There was heavy drinking, along with all that happens when drunkenness prevails.

Steve liked his birth father, got to know family members, and stayed somewhat connected until Paul's death. He traveled from Missouri to Las Vegas with his nephew Ben and Ben's wife and baby to visit Paul when he was terminally ill. Steve was sad to see his birth father pass away because he had not taken very good care of his body. Steve still has his second family, which consists of half brothers Dave and Kevin and his half sister Kathy and their children. He has a special relationship with Ben, who is Kathy's son.

The way Steve learned that he was adopted wasn't entirely planned. It didn't happen while he and his adoptive father and mother sat at the table and discussed it over a cup of coffee. Family members knew he was adopted, and several had pressed Patty, his adoptive mother, to tell Steve about his adoption. When Steve was adopted by Bryce and Patty Hastings in 1961, the social worker insisted it was better if the child was raised with no knowledge of the adoption. Patty now believes that this approach was wrong. It became more and more evident to her that Steve should know that he was adopted.

One day, as teenagers do, Steve ruffled her feathers in a disagreement, and she said to him, "I am not your real mother." Steve says, "From that moment on, I was very surprised, even in shock." He wanted to know about his birth mother. Patty was able to show him pictures, as his mother was Patty's sister.

Patty's sister, Linda, was a beautiful, intelligent girl. She was adorable and highly likeable. As a teenager, she'd had many friends. But then schizophrenia set in. By the time she was twenty years old, she was having a very rough time with mental illness. When Naomi, Patty and Linda's mother, realized that Linda was pregnant, a decision was made for her immediate future. As soon as Linda started to show that she was expecting a baby, she was sent to Booth Memorial Home (also known as Booth Memorial Hospital) for unwed mothers in St. Louis.

In the late 1950s and 60s, there were a number of good homes, and Booth Memorial Home provided a nurturing, healthy start for Linda's baby. In those days, the pregnant teenager just disappeared from the family for a while. Later, the teenager returned home, and life went on. Booth Memorial Home normally arranged for a closed adoption and placed the infant in a family. However, this time the home called Linda's parents and said that the baby was about to be born. Would they please come and get Linda and the baby?

Linda loved her baby and wouldn't place him for adoption. She was religious and knew that Steve was a gift from God, and she would not give him up. Linda tried for six months to care for the child, but she had a very rough time. There was no help from Steve's father, Paul, at that time. Paul already had a wife and four children. Linda had to do this by herself.

Patty saw her sister struggling. She did what any sister would have done and offered to help. The situation was worsened because Patty had just had a miscarriage, and the doctor told her that she couldn't have any more children. Emotions were running wild for both women. Patty was mourning for her child. She was married, had a husband with a good job, and wanted a baby but couldn't have one. When she saw how much her sister loved her baby but couldn't take care of him, she offered her help, even saying that she and Bryce would adopt Steve if Linda wanted that.

Steve realizes that he might not have been born if his birth mother had not known God and had not known how to love. She had been desperate and could have taken a different path. She could have believed that the baby inside her was not really a life.

One day, Linda, realizing that the care of the baby was too difficult for her as a single mother, approached Patty's house. She rang the doorbell and handed Steve to Patty. It was Steve's six-month birthday, and he was getting a new mother. Bryce and Patty went through a private adoption, with a social worker coming to the house once a month to see if everything was okay. They were close to getting everything finalized, when Patty became pregnant.

She was terrified, fearing that the authorities would take Steve and give him to some other family to adopt. Patty had been telling the truth about not being able to have children, but it sure didn't look like it now. The courts did allow them to adopt Steve, and they had a new birth certificate made out for him with the name Steven Mitchell Hastings. Not long after the adoption, Steve's brother was born, joining an older sister to complete the Hastings family.

Linda continued to struggle with her mental illness and eventually decided to end her life when Steve was about two years old. She tried suicide several times before she succeeded. This was only part of the struggles in Steve's birth family during his growing up years.

The adoption was a bright spot for Steve. He says he is fortunate that Bryce and Patty raised him in a stable, quiet home. His life could have been a rocky road of trials and tribulations. He came to know his birth father, and he knows his birth mother died on September 9, 1963. He is thankful that his mother, Linda Susan McFarland, gave him life. He is glad that she "did what she did" when she put him in Patty's hands. He grew up thinking he was just a normal kid. He never worried, thought about, or discussed being adopted. He was raised in a nice home and was loved and well cared for by a mother and a nice, well-centered father. He even knew that his middle name was supposed to be Michael instead of Mitchell, but it was no big deal to him that it was wrong on the birth certificate. Bryce and Patty were his parents, and he was always called Steve.

Steve became very close to his grandmother, Naomi, Patty and Linda's mother. He knew she was emotionally compromised by something. Eventually he came to know that she had become pregnant at the age of fifteen and that she and Lewis McFarland had been forced to get married. You know, those old "shotgun" weddings happened in many families. Some thought at the time that this was the only way to settle the condition of pregnancy. The family believes now that this is not a good solution, as marriage is very difficult without love.

Naomi clung to Steve, and he loved it, even before he knew that Naomi was his grandmother—not only once, but twice. She had lost her daughter Linda, but she still had Linda's baby, Steve. Because of the secret, private adoption, she couldn't talk to Steve about all these things. Sometime in the 1970s Lewis McFarland, her husband, also committed suicide. He was a person who invested people's money, but this was long before people went to school and became licensed to do this work. He had invested poorly and had lost everyone's money, including his own. Steve was there for Naomi at that time, along with her friend Ellie. Ellie was the one who removed Lewis's possessions from the house, as Naomi wasn't able to deal with everything. Her losses were difficult to bear, and she had bouts of depression.

Naomi had to go to work after the loss of her husband in order to support herself. She found work in a hospital. Steve was pleased that they gave her a good deal: if she worked for them for ten years, they would give her a retirement pension. She lived in a trailer, and Steve and Ellie visited her often. She eventually moved to a fifteen-story assisted-living building. Steve frequented her apartment often up until her death.

As a child, Steve attended Sunday School in a Methodist church in St. Louis, but he wandered away from any religious affiliation, until one day some Jehovah's Witnesses came by his house and invited him to worship. His attention was again turned to his faith in God. A man named Cliff Hurlburt mentored him.

One night, Steve was playing his piano with his window open at about two or three in the morning, and he saw a figure watching him from the window. He became a little worried that it was a neighbor who was going to ask him to quiet down, or the police who were going to give him a warning for disturbing the peace. The man at the window was Patrick Brown. Steve asked him to come in.

Patrick Brown had a compulsion to walk the streets, and because of the sound of Steve's music through the window, Steve met Patrick. Patrick had a friend named Keith Green, who taught Steve about Jesus and about being saved through Jesus' blood shed on the cross for him. Keith Green could sing like Billy Joel and Elton John. He was that good. Keith Green drew people to God with his work because he used words from the Bible like "alive in Christ" or "to be dead to self." His relationship with Keith Green inspired Steve to write and play Christian music.

Patrick Brown was also the connection that brought Pastor David Evans into Steve's life on the day that David was ordained at Patrick's church. Steve met Pastor Evans that Sunday and followed him to the Gateway Bible Fellowship, where Steve ministered through music.

Pastor Evans guided Steve along his faith journey and baptized him as an adult in a river south and west of St. Louis, Missouri.

Steve has inspired others to accept Jesus' free gift of eternal life and to accept Jesus as their Lord and Savior through his DVD entitled *His Free Gift*. Steve is tremendously gifted with musical talent. He can play any song by ear. This means that if he has heard the song, he can play it on the piano. His fingers move quickly, and he repeats what he has heard. It is a joy to hear and see such talent.

Steve played the piano at the reception for his brother's wedding, and everyone enjoyed it immensely. On his DVD, recorded in 1998, Steve sang and played songs that portrayed his deep faith in his Savior. Steve wrote the songs and music himself. In Steve Hastings' work, like Keith Green's, he uses words from the Bible. He used the words in Psalm 51:10: "Create in me a pure heart, O God, and renew a steadfast spirit within me." Songs that Steve performed on his DVD are listed below, and you can see other phrases that come directly from the Bible:

- Psalm 23
- Create in Me a Clean Heart
- He Did It All for Me
- This Is the Day
- God Is So Willing
- Morning Has Broken
- His Free Gift
- He's the Way
- King of Kings
- Jesus Is the Rock
- My Eyes Are Dry

Steve felt that Keith Green's music was amazing and that it actually drew people away from the desires of their flesh. After listening to Keith's music for some time, people were actually able to follow Christ and do things they normally would not have been able to do. Steve refers to Philippians 4:13: "I can do everything through him who gives me strength." When Keith's songs, with such strong biblical words, were played over and over, they developed into something more, like a final completion. Steve related that final completion to working a muscle and seeing it get stronger. While playing "Go Tell It on the Mountain," Steve experienced this type of drawing close to God, and the music became a strong form of worship. Because Steve wanted others to experience this closeness to God, he was inspired by Keith Green and used his talents to play the piano for Gateway Bible Fellowship church in the downtown St. Louis area twice a week for years. He still plays there sometimes.

Steve believes the words in Hebrews 4:12: "For the word of God is living and active. Sharper than any double-edged sword, it penetrates even to dividing soul and spirit, joints and marrow; it judges the thoughts and attitudes of the heart."

Turning to You

Steve's mother Patty says, "If you are not ready to raise your baby, someone else is. If you have to choose between abortion, forced marriage, raising the baby when you're not ready, and adoption, *adoption* is the best answer." Steve's adoption provided a stable home for his childhood, and it paved the way for him to become a compassionate adult. He has overcome the struggles known in his birth family, and he is a truly wonderful person who is serving others. "You, dear children, are from God and have overcome them, because the one who is in you is greater than the one who is in the world" (1 John 4:4).

Prayer

Dear Lord, we thank You for parents who adopt children, for connecting us to people in our lives who influence us, and for teaching us love in Your Scriptures. Amen.

3

Action of Love by One Adopted

Alex Lentfer

Alexander Mikhail Lentfer was adopted from Moscow, Russia, in 1999. His adoptive parents lived in Texas but moved to Kansas before he came to live with them. Most of the adoption papers were processed through the Texas courts. He arrived in the United States and went to Kansas to live with his new parents at the tender age of fifteen months. He learned to walk while his adoptive parents were still in Russia completing the Russian side of the adoption. Baby House #14 in Moscow had a very accommodating director, who allowed the parents to take Alexander to their flat. They walked him back and forth in the hall, and soon he was taking steps on his own.

Before Alex was two years old, his parents took him to Texas to get his citizenship papers and to finalize his adoption papers. President Bill Clinton had signed a law that allowed all foreign adopted children to become American citizens. Alex was baptized in a Methodist church in the Dallas metro area and remains a Methodist today. Alex joined an older sister in his Kansas home.

The reason Alex's parents adopted him was because his mother had had five miscarriages after carrying their daughter. They didn't believe that they could have another child. They named their new son Alexander Mikhail Lentfer. His Russian name was Igor Mikhailovic Muralev. They chose the name because Alexander was a name they wanted for a son, and his adoptive father is named Michael. Mikhailovic means son of Michael in Russian.

Alex has always known the story of his adoption and has never had a problem with it. On occasion, he has wondered about his biological parents. There was little information left at the hospital with Alex when he was born and consequently taken to Baby House #14. He has embraced his Russian heritage by attending FRUA (Families for Russian and Ukrainian Adoption) events in Kansas City.

It was disheartening for Alex when Vladimir Putin, president of Russia, stopped American adoptions from Russia. He realized that if this ban had occurred before his own adoption, he might never have come to America. Putin made this decision because some adopted Russian children had been abused. In reality, there have been very few such cases, considering the thousands of children who have found homes in America. Alex believes his American family is a better fit for him than his biological family would have been.

There is a special way that Alex protests abortion because he understands that it might have happened to him. He is thankful that his mother gave him life. He gave up his favorite beverage, root beer, and proudly tells those who offer him the drink about his position. He feels a sense of pride and joy when he sees billboards of a baby saying, "Take my hand, not my life" or "It's a baby, not a choice."

Alex takes his commitment to oppose abortion to another level, in that he has made a choice not to have sexual relations until he marries. He does this to prevent a child of his own from being born without knowing his biological parents. Except when he is playing football, Alex wears a ring at all times to show this commitment. He receives criticism, but he defends his position and has some friends who support him. He believes there are many positive results from making this decision. It helps him to avoid some unwanted circumstances.

At sixteen years old, Alex has been able to attend a top school district in the nation and has received a world-class education. He partakes in athletic competition such as football and rugby, which might not have been possible with his biological parents. In 2013 his football team won the state championship, a feat that gives him great pleasure. These activities have allowed him to be part of a small group of people fighting for one common goal. He has learned to set aside differences to make the team better. Sports have helped him to understand that a person has to put in an immense amount of effort in order to succeed.

Alex has enjoyed and learned much from his Church of the Resurrection mission trips around the United States, and he was confirmed in the church as a sixth grader. He plays the piano and guitar and knows how to play tennis. He enjoys family gatherings. He has talked to ordained ministers about a possible career in church clergy work.

Alex believes that no matter what has happened or what we have done on earth, we can still receive God's blessing if we ask for it. He also believes that what we do on earth is important, and that accepting Christ as our Savior affects what happens to our souls after life. He believes that just trying to have as much fun as possible is not God's purpose for us.

Some of Alex's favorite verses are found in Revelation 22:12–16:

> Behold, I am coming soon! My reward is with me, and I will give to everyone according to what he has done. I am the Alpha and the Omega, the First and the Last, the Beginning and the End. Blessed are those who wash their robes, that they may have the right to the tree of life and may go through the gates into the city. Outside are the dogs, those who practice magic arts, the sexually immoral, the murderers, the idolaters

and everyone who loves and practices falsehood. I, Jesus, have sent my angel to give you this testimony for the churches. I am the Root and the Offspring of David, and the bright Morning Star.

Turning to You

What about you? Can you make commitments and stick to them like Alex does? He knows what he opposes, and he isn't afraid to tell others. He understands forgiveness and knows that Jesus will bring His faithful home to Him. He wishes to set personal boundaries and to be in control of his actions, knowing that they have eternal consequences.

Prayer

Dear Lord, lift us up to praise You, Your commandments, and Your promises. Thank You for all of our experiences, which make us grow and become useful to You. In Jesus' name, amen.

4

She Found Love at Every Address

Pat Sim

This is a unique story about being adopted twice.
God gave Pat a wonderful temperament, lots of skills, a desire and capabilities that made learning easy, friends in every situation, and what we all need: love. Her biological mother left her at a hospital in Omaha, Nebraska, in the year 1928. Pat holds no grudge against her birth mother, as she has never known what was her mother's predicament at the time. "Therefore let us stop passing judgment on one another" (Romans 14:13).

The first mother she knew was fifty-five years old when she and her husband adopted Pat. Diabetes had taken a toll on this mother's health. Pat may have been about three years old at the time. She remembers the adoption but knows nothing about her baby and toddler years. Her second mother, who was forty-seven years old when she adopted Pat, struggled with many issues. Pat absorbed the love from each of her adoptive mothers, even under hard circumstances. Her fathers worked hard and took Pat many interesting places and cared deeply for her.

Pat's first parents were very poor; they lived in apartments close to the railroad tracks. There were no regular playmates, as Pat was often in the apartment, helping her ill mother. She remembers standing in the bread line, taking a bath once a week, and watching the circus set up in their backyard. Up the street was where *Omaha Bee News*, a pioneer newspaper founded May 8, 1871, was printed. Pat possessed two dresses. The highlight of her day was when she went out with her dad, James Clarence McKay. He would take her to the store and allow her to buy five cents' worth of penny candy. James was fifty-seven years old, and Pat remembers that people always said something to him about having his granddaughter along with him.

Before Pat started going to school, James taught her to read. Imagine the attention given to her by this father as she learned to read so young. At home, she had a little book about geography, and she memorized all the states of the United States of America and their capital cities before entering her first classroom. Pat loved school. Because of her capabilities, she excelled despite changing schools and teachers on a regular basis. Here is a list of the schools Pat attended:

- Mason Elementary, 1012 S. 24th St., Omaha, Nebraska
- Rose Hill South Elementary, 5605 Corby St., Omaha, Nebraska
- Central Park Elementary, 4904 N. 42nd St., Omaha, Nebraska
- Dundee Elementary, 310 N. 51st St., Omaha, Nebraska
- Walnut Hills Elementary, 4355 Charles St., Omaha, Nebraska
- Conway Junior High, Conway, Arkansas (Some schools started junior high earlier.)
- Loveland Elementary, 8201 Pacific St., Omaha, Nebraska
- Pierce, Nebraska, county seat of Pierce County (population fewer than two thousand)

- Woodrow Wilson Junior High, Glendale, California
- Glendale High, Glendale, California
- Withrow High, Cincinnati, Ohio (the twenty-eighth largest US city)

Pat's names reflect her background and all the many changes in her life. She started out being Patricia Ann McKay. Pat's first mother's health problems became worse, and she spent time at the hospital, which has since become the University of Nebraska Medical Center. At the tender age of an elementary school student, Pat was alone with her mother at the Douglas County Hospital when she died. Unable to know exactly what had happened, Pat remembers clearly going for help.

The death of the only mother she had known made changes in her life. James could not care for her during the day, so he placed her at Minerva Cottage for Girls, which cost about three dollars a week. This took a toll on their finances, but he had no choice. Most of the twelve to fourteen children at the Cottage were from troubled homes, but a few had been taken from abusive homes.

Pat felt lucky that she had a father who cared about her. She now believes that James was responsible for her survival. She remembers that every Thursday he found a pay phone and called her at the Cottage. On Saturday afternoons, he picked her up and cooked her dinner, and together they went to see movies at the old Orpheum Theatre. They attended church on Sunday morning.

At the Cottage, Pat learned how to expertly clean a room. She made the back porch spic and span. When the Cottage was shown to outsiders, they always picked the back porch because they knew it would be clean. Her friend Betty Jean Rowe cleaned the living room, and Pat always hoped she would be promoted and be allowed to clean the living room, but it never happened.

While Pat was still in elementary school, her beloved father died. She remembers people being kind to her. She loved her teacher Mrs. Thickson at Rose Hill School. At the city health department,

Dr. Pinto did minor surgery on her infected finger. The doctor remembered her at Christmas and sent her five dollars. Later, she had her tonsils out, and all the people at the hospital were good to her. The Hattie B. Munro Home took the younger children, including Pat, when Minerva Cottage was divided into two groups. Later, she was in the foster care system while attending Central Park Elementary school.

Her memories of that time are of living in a little house with Mrs. Carlson and her family. Her teacher, Miss Nevin, suggested to the school that Pat be skipped to sixth grade, which promptly happened. The caseworker took her to a big house where a lady made and sold canapés (a small prepared and usually decorated food, held in the fingers and often eaten in one bite) for hors d'oeuvres. While there, Pat ate eight or nine of them. Her appetite surprised the lady. She spent one night at a home by the Field Club Golf Course and remembers breaking some perfume bottles.

The caseworker took Pat and her friend Betty Jean to a home near Irvington where some foster parents ran an ice cream place. The couple was looking for a child to adopt, and they picked Betty Jean. Pat was obviously hurt by their choice, but it was just another part of her life that she learned to put aside so she could move forward. Perhaps memories of her father helped her to go on. She missed the ice cream.

Mr. and Mrs. Walter Black lived in the Dundee area of Omaha and took Pat in—overnight first, and then for a few weekends. They attended Dundee Presbyterian Church with Pat. This home was where Pat learned table manners. "You don't take your mouth to the fork, you take the fork to the mouth," she was told. "Break the bread into four pieces and butter one at a time. Don't saw your meat; cut it. Keep your left hand in your lap." These were words she heard all the time.

Mrs. Black was a fanatic about a clean house, so Pat picked up some more cleaning tips, some of which she still uses. The Blacks also took her to get ice cream. One day they asked Pat if she would like to live with them for six months to see how well they adjusted to each other. If all went well, they would adopt Pat. This sounded good to Pat, so she moved in with them and went to Dundee Elementary School. They gave her a bicycle, and she rode through an underpass to school.

While Pat lived with the Blacks, she learned how to iron. She was taught on pleated shorts. This was definitely not polyester or permanent press material. It must have been untreated cotton, and the job took a whole evening to do. She must have pleased them because the Blacks adopted Pat at when she was eleven years old, and she became Patricia Merrily Black. Her second set of parents were about forty-one and forty-five years old when the adoption took place.

Pat had two bedrooms assigned to her in her new home, and she kept them very clean. She loved being part of a family again. Her new father took her on her biggest trip ever—to a University of Nebraska football game. The great times lasted for a while, and then World War II came. Her new father was sent to Camp Robinson with the Nebraska National Guard. Pat and her mother went to Conway, Arkansas, to live, which was about twenty-eight miles from Camp Robinson. They got along well, but soon it was evident that the adoption and being separated from her husband had put strain on Mrs. Black. She was a very precise person who had not been around children much before. One time, Pat cleaned the bathtub so clean after her bath that she was sent back to take another bath, as it looked as if Pat had lied.

With the Black adoption, Pat gained grandparents in Pierce, Nebraska. They were unfriendly to Pat because they'd wanted their daughter to adopt someone else. After Pat had grown up, married, and had her own children, the grandmother told her, "Can you ever forgive me for how I treated you?" As expected, because of Pat's unusual gifts, she was able to forgive. Some things are never forgotten in life, so they couldn't be undone years later.

Before the United States entered the war, Pat had a wonderful trip to Mexico with her second father and mother. When they came back, they lived in the Flat Iron Hotel at 91st and Pacific Streets while they looked for housing in Omaha. Pat attended Loveland Elementary School for the eighth grade. Their home at this time was new and beautiful, as Mrs. Black's decorating skills were excellent. The war took her father away to Santa Monica, California. Mrs. Black knew it would be best for Pat to stay in Omaha until she graduated from elementary school.

Eventually Mrs. Black had to sell their home, and she and Pat went to live with the grandmother at Pierce, Nebraska. Her father worked out a way to rent an apartment in Glendale, California, and they went to live with him. He was always finding ways to help Pat. She was sent to Woodrow Wilson Junior High for ninth grade, and she liked it a lot. Living with her dad again was very special for Pat. And as she always did, Pat made many friends.

Things kept changing, as Mr. Black quickly moved up the line with promotions. When he was sent to Fresno, California, Pat and her mother were alone again. Pat tried to be a better child. She was living in California close to Hollywood, but she stayed away from smoking and drinking. She spent four weeks at summer camp and loved it. She returned to the camp for a second year and worked in the clothing unit, ironing for eight to ten weeks. The third year, she spent the summer as a junior counselor.

When Pat was a senior in high school, her father came home after being at the Battle of the Bulge. In the bitter winter on December 16, 1944, when World War II was all but over, the German army launched a counteroffensive that was intended to cut through the Allied forces. This battle is known as the greatest battle in American history. Mr. Black did not come home alone. He brought home a sixth-grade boy.

Change continued in Pat's life as she adjusted to her father being home and a new child in the house. The family moved to Cincinnati, Ohio, right in the middle of her senior year of high school. This time the move was hard, as she had more trouble making friends. The seniors at her new school had their friends picked and were preparing for their future. Being good at sports helped her to make some friends.

Pat graduated from, and has been an instructor at, the University of Nebraska. She has mentored many, many youngsters. She now serves on the Foster Care Review Board for the state of Nebraska. She holds no ill feelings for the caretakers and parents in her life, as she knows they did the best they could with the information they had. She accepted the love given to her by parents, teachers, and others. And she has passed that love on to others.

Turning to You

Can you imagine changing schools, homes, and environment throughout your growing-up years? Pat's two mothers and two fathers accepted a child into their homes in spite of poverty, illness, advanced age, and eventually a world war. They provided all that Pat needed. Could we have given of ourselves in that way? Would we have had the perseverance Pat had and have grown up to teach others? "We rejoice in the hope of the glory of God. Not only so, but we rejoice in our sufferings, because we know that suffering produces perseverance; perseverance, character, and character, hope. And hope does not disappoint us, because God has poured out his love into our hearts by the Holy Spirit, whom he has given us" (Romans 5:2b–5).

Prayer

Dear Lord, help us to be patient, kind, and nonjudgmental. Pat could do this even when immersed in hard times, death, depression, war, dislocation, and relocation. She never lost hope. She learned to love. "Above all, love each other deeply, because love covers over a multitude of sins" (1 Peter 4:8). Thank You for her survival and for all the times she helped others as a caring and loving adult. Amen.

Reason 2

Children Are an Unbelievable Blessing

5

Finding Love after the Years

Sue Anne Philson

"I don't know what to say," wrote Sue Anne. She had been thinking about writing to her biological mother for most of her life. She wrote, "I have spent most of my life wondering if I am anything like you. Now, from your letter and photos, I see that we are alike, and it is a little scary." She went on to tell about her adoptive family and their support in helping her find her birth mother. She told her mother about her siblings, her hometown, her high school activities, and being homecoming queen. What mother would not melt upon hearing about the wonderful life she had given her daughter through adoption?

In her letter, Sue Anne told her mother about her loving husband and her life as an adult. When she met her birth mother, Sue Anne did not have any children, so her biological mother was able to experience the births of her two biological grandchildren. What a joy!

Although Sue Anne had a good family and life, she felt that she had worked hard all of her life to be someone that her biological mom would be proud to say she'd brought into this world. That didn't mean there weren't times when she felt very angry, but as an adult, Sue Anne realized the gift she'd been given through adoption. Now Sue Anne was ready to meet the one who had given her life.

Sue Anne's birth mother was only sixteen when she gave birth. She was like Sue Anne in that she had good grades, participated in lots of school activities, and was a queen at the Mardi Gras in Omaha, Nebraska. Then there was dance, something that both women loved. The possibility of meeting gained momentum every time Sue Anne learned more about her birth mother. The United Catholic Social Services had a letter from Sue Anne's mother stating that she wanted to be contacted for a reunion with her natural daughter if Jill (the name she gave Sue Anne) would contact the agency at age twenty-five.

The meeting time came, and Sue Anne received a letter from her birth mom. She asked how Sue Anne had been doing for the last twenty-five years. The birth mom revealed a touching moment of love about their first thirty minutes together when Sue Anne was one day old. She gathered Sue Anne into her arms on the sly, which put the head nurse into a tizzy. The adoption plan had already been signed. The young mother had wanted to keep the baby, but she understood that it was the right decision to place Sue Anne into a complete family with mature, loving parents. After telling Sue Anne in the letter that she was nervous, her birth mother proceeded to tell Sue Anne how much she loved her.

This love of Sue Anne's birth mother was realized in her thinking about the baby every day and in asking the Lord to keep Sue Anne safe, healthy, and happy. Being a Christian, this birth mother also prayed for Sue Anne to have a relationship with our Lord. If you can believe it, both women had cocker spaniel dogs for pets. After finding out about the cocker spaniel, Sue Anne read in the letter that she was an only child. Her birth mother had never had any more babies. She was married and had two stepchildren.

Then came the kicker: Sue Anne's birth mother was creative. She was a graphic designer. She loved needlework and had even made a baby blanket that she'd sent to Sue Anne. The interesting part about this is that Sue Anne was a very creative person as well. She made the summer Bible school at her church fun for all the kids and teachers. She could create anything. This was an early bonding item for Sue Anne, knowing that she shared this talent with her birth mother. Another wonderful, inspiring piece of information for Sue Anne was the knowledge that her birth mother was a Christian who practiced her faith and worshipped often.

Sue Anne's birth mother expressed sorrow for any pain she may have caused Sue Anne in her growing up years, and she asked forgiveness for bad choices and poor judgment. She hoped that Sue Anne was wiser than she. At thirty-nine years of age, Sue Anne was comfortable enough with her story and the reunion with her mother that she was able to tell others about her experience. She even told of her childhood fantasies about being with her biological parents, living in a huge castle, being a princess with servants, and having a twin who was trying to find her.

In reality, Sue Anne had a wonderful childhood and an adoptive mother whom she loves equally with her newfound biological mother. Sue Anne knows that her life would have been different—but perhaps not better—if her biological parents had married and raised her. She believes that God had a plan for her, and she quotes Jeremiah 29:11: "'For I know the plans I have for you,' declares the Lord, 'plans to prosper you and not to harm you, plans to give you hope and a future.'"

The family members who adopted Sue Anne were very serious people, and sometimes she wondered why none of them joked around or were creative like she was. Sue Anne says, "Being adopted is not the same as being born into a family. It's is not better or worse, just different." Sue Anne knew she didn't have a family history like others she knew, and at times she didn't know who she really was. When doing homework for genetics, she borrowed her adoptive family's heritage, but she soon realized that the process didn't work for her. After meeting her birth mother, she was able to say that her family can be traced back to Elvis and Thomas Jefferson. Sue Anne and her husband, Brad, were able to go to a Corrigan (her birth family name) family reunion in Ireland.

Sue Anne was not reunited with her birth mother for ten long months after she contacted Catholic Social Services. The waiting was hard, and she never once doubted that she wanted to know her birth mother. Some members of both families feared the worst, thinking the person they hadn't met was just interested in money. Sue Anne learned that her mother was Sandee Jenkins, who wrote a letter in February that didn't reach her until September. After writing several times, Sue Anne was ready to physically meet Sandee. She was anxious and nervous but ready to see her birth mother.

Finally the call came. Sue Anne experienced tears of pain and joy. Sandee announced first that she would fly to Lincoln, Nebraska, to see Sue Anne and her family. Sue Anne's job took her to the airport also, but the plane arrived two hours late. She had to have her husband go to the airport and meet Sandee.

The customers Sue Anne had taken to Chicago were very excited to be a part of Sandee's and Sue Anne's reunion. They told everyone on the plane that Sandee and Sue Anne were to meet for the first time. The attendants told the pilots, who made an announcement of the meeting and presented Sue Anne with a bottle of champagne. They made her promise to be the last person off the plane so everyone could witness the reunion. I know this story sounds like a soap opera, but this was a big, big deal. Sue Anne refused the invitation to call the news station, but she found herself surrounded by a crowd as she saw Brad smiling and Sandee running toward her. They hugged and cried. The people clapped and cheered, making it a great experience.

Can you imagine the feeling of seeing someone who resembles you so much for the first time and knowing that she was your birth mother, the person who gave you life? Not only do the two women look alike, but they are the same height. They also act, think, and laugh alike and have the same weird sense of humor. Even their choice of eyeglasses is similar. Their haircuts are the same and their hair is dyed the same color. Sue Anne is a strong case for genetics over environment. Sandee's husband said, "Why, they are identical. If you know Sandee, you know Sue Anne." Sue Anne herself says, "We spent no time together for twenty-six years, yet we are like identical twins."

It seemed that this reunion was to be enjoyed by all. In Sue Anne's hometown of Stuart, Nebraska, six hundred people came to the church pancake feed to meet Sandee. Sue Anne saw how tired Sandee was after talking to every one of the parishioners. The reunion involved a lot of people, but the day they met is solidly Sue Anne's and Sandee's greatest day. The two of them continue to meet each other four times a year and sometimes more. They talk on the phone and e-mail as if they had been together for the past twenty-five years. This has been going on for the last fifteen years.

If you like this story, please be sure to read Sandee Jenkins' story also, which follows this story.

Turning to You

If you and a family member have been separated for a long time, you might want to schedule a reunion. Not all reunions are like Sandee's and Sue Anne's, but relationships within families and adoptive families are important. Pray, and your prayers may be answered. "So do not fear, for I am with you; do not be dismayed, for I am your God. I will strengthen you and help you; I will uphold you with my righteous right hand" (Isaiah 41:10).

Sue Anne says to pregnant women who are undecided about what to do, "Will you choose to do something you think is acceptable because everyone else is doing it—or because it lives up to God's laws? Are you justifying your actions by man's standards or God's? Why compare man's justification with God's? Life is precious."

Sandra Hilsabeck

Prayer

　　Dear Father in heaven, thank You for the relationship renewed in this story. Please bless Sandee and Sue Anne as they go forward. Thank You for Sue Anne's two families and the love they share unselfishly. We also thank You that Sandee and Sue Anne are sisters in Christ, which binds them even closer. We all wait, as Sue Anne did, for Paul's words in Romans 8:23 to come true: "But we ourselves, who have the firstfruits of the Spirit, groan inwardly as we wait eagerly for our adoption as sons, the redemption of our bodies." Your willingness to adopt us to be heirs with Christ shows us the true love a parent can give. Amen.

6

Love at First Sight

Sandee Jenkins

Sandee Jenkins, Sue Anne Philson's birth mother, wrote, "The hole in my heart can only be filled by you." The "you" is Sue Anne, whom she placed for adoption twenty-six years ago. Sandee realizes now that it was not a mistake to give birth to her daughter and then give her up for adoption. The hole has been there a long time, but now it is filled by a lovely daughter.

Sandee answered these questions from the bottom of her heart.

What would be the most wonderful gift you could receive? Why? "I have it already. My life is complete. I have a relationship with my long-lost only daughter. I have the Lord in my heart. Others will pass away, but I have my rock to lean on."

Tell me about a time when God answered a specific prayer for you. "That's easy. I prayed for twenty-six years that God would bring my daughter and me together. He did. I prayed that she would be safe and healthy. She was. I prayed for twenty-six years that she would be in a happy, secure family with lots of love. She was. Thank You, Lord, for answered prayer!"

What is your most vivid memory of being pregnant? "I remember sitting in the bath, stroking my swelled tummy with the warm water, talking to my baby. I took long walks near Mamaw and Papaw's house. I spent a lot of time alone. I read *Gone with the Wind* during the day and dreamed about it at night. I mostly spent time wishing things could have been different, that I could have been married and kept Sue Anne and lived happily ever after."

Did you choose the baby's name? If so, why? "I named her Jill Ann because I loved the name. I always thought it was funny that her adoptive parents named her Sue Anne. It was so close."

What would you do differently if you could? "I'd do some things differently, but then my daughter wouldn't be here—so never mind! Mostly I would have listened more to my elders and teachers. I would have kept my body chaste and treated it like the temple of the Holy Spirit that it is."

What was the hardest thing you ever had to do? "Release my precious little baby girl to adoptive parents when I was only sixteen. I'll never do anything harder than that. It took superhuman strength, and it was the ultimate sacrifice."

This birth mother, Sandee, had only thirty minutes to hold her daughter Sue Anne in the hospital, as it was against the rules for mothers who had signed adoption papers. She wanted to keep her baby forever. A day never went by that she didn't think about her little one. Sandee married and had stepchildren, but Sue Anne was her only child by birth. Sandee was a dancer and worked in creative, artistic jobs. She liked needlework, especially cross stitch and needlepoint. During her pregnancy, she made her baby a blanket and sent it with her to her new home. Best of all, she claims to have a wonderful relationship with the Lord. Sandee was one of seven girls in her family.

Sandee is ecstatic about having her daughter in her life as an adult, but this end result didn't come about easily. It was horrible coming up with the courage to tell her parents that she was pregnant. Her mother was angry and told her father. Her parents decided that she would adopt the baby out, and they sent her to her grandmother's house a couple of months later. There were no vacancies in the home for unwed mothers in Florida where they tried to place her. Sandee's grandmother convinced her mom to let the youngsters get married. Once they got permission, the young man missed coming to see Sandee twice. After a while, Sandee walked to a great aunt's house, made a phone call to him, and called the wedding off. This was actually a big benefit to Sandee. She understood this later when she found out that he had another girlfriend who was pregnant too.

The wait for the baby's arrival began, and Sandee gave birth to Sue Anne on November 6, 1967. Soon afterward, she flew back to Omaha, and everyone pretended that nothing had happened. The subject was taboo. Sandee went back to high school and graduated with her class, with honors. She was blessed with being elected vice president of her senior class. In college, Sandee danced ballet, tap, and modern jazz, and she taught it to younger girls.

By age eighteen, Sandee was mature. She moved into an apartment and soon departed for Washington, DC, on a dance scholarship. Her dance opportunities took her to several states, but she always sent a letter to Catholic Charities, telling them where she had moved, in case her daughter would want to meet her. The adorable baby was never far from her mind. When Sandee was engaged to be married, she was very open with her fiancé Mike about having a daughter who had been placed for adoption.

It was only about four years after she married and became the stepmother of two children that she received a phone call from Catholic Charities and learned that her daughter was trying to find her. Photos and letters were exchanged, and Sandee felt the same excitement Sue Anne did about the pending reunion of mother and daughter. They talked for an hour and a half on their first phone call.

Sandee flew into Lincoln to meet Sue Anne, and no one was there to meet the plane. She had been so nervous and so excited in the little commuter plane, but then Sue Anne wasn't there. Had she misinterpreted the conversations? Sandee saw a handsome man coming toward her. It was Brad, Sue Anne's husband, followed by her sister and her family who live in Lincoln. Brad told her the plane bringing Sue Anne back to Lincoln was late. They watched as the late plane arrived and saw a hundred passengers file out before Sue Anne. The passengers had heard about Sue Anne's reunion and wanted to watch. Sandee handed Sue Anne a teddy bear that Sandee had kept since her pregnancy days, which caused everyone to clap and laugh.

The reunion group traveled to the small town where Brad and Sue Anne lived to meet her family. This proceeded to be a pancake supper for most of the town. Sandee was amazed at how friendly everyone, including Sue Anne's adoptive parents, sister, and brother were to her. The pains of separation began to fade. The hurt and fear of telling her parents about her teen pregnancy seemed so long ago. The joy of talking about her daughter without the subject being taboo was enormous. Sue Anne was able to enjoy both her families, and she finally had her own genetic history. The fears of both families were dissipated.

Turning to You

Remember that the search for birth parents is normally to give understanding to curiosity. It reflects the need to know one's roots and is a search for heritage. Most of the time, the adopted child wants to thank the birth parents. Even when a reunion does not provide closeness between the adopted child and birth parents, the reunion does answer questions and provides an end to the search. Most of the time, both parties are blessed in some way. Sandee says, "The hole in my heart can only be filled by you, my one and only daughter by birth." "Sons are a heritage from the LORD, children a reward from him" (Psalm 127:3).

Prayer

Thank You, Lord, for the love given by adoptive parents and for the agencies that help place babies when birth parents cannot provide a home for them. Thank You, Lord, for Your great plan for families. We pray that each and every baby may be provided with a mother and a father. Amen.

7

Comfortable in a Loving Home

Heidi Stark

Heidi always knew she was adopted, and there was nothing uncomfortable about it. This was a fact. People would tell her it was neat that she had been chosen and that it made her a special child. Her brother, Jason, remembers being told at the age of six or seven that he was adopted. Heidi never considered it necessary to find her birth mother. However, Jason, who is three and a half years older than Heidi, had other thoughts.

After Jason was grown and before he married, he decided he needed to know who his birth mother was. He learned that Susan, a teen from Michigan, had been sent away to live with her aunt and uncle until she gave birth to her baby in Kansas City, Kansas. This plan was not Susan's. She tried to change the scenario and escaped from the hospital with the baby in her arms and five dollars in her possession. People from the hospital found her in the parking lot and said she could not leave with the baby. Soon a cab took her to the airport, and she flew back home without her baby. The topic of this baby didn't arise again for many long years. The whole subject was swept under the rug.

After years of searching for his birth mother with Lutheran Family Social Services, miscellaneous state departments, and various investigators—to no avail—Jason found his original birth certificate in Topeka at the State Bureau of Vital Statistics. It took only five minutes. He was totally surprised by this turn of events, as he had simply been driving by, said "what the heck," and had gone inside to talk with the authorities. His mother was from Kalamazoo, Michigan. He went to the library and got a copy of the Kalamazoo phone book and copied down all the phone numbers of everyone with the same last name. He called everyone on the list, with no luck—until the very last name, which happened to be his grandpa. Jason didn't let him know who he was at the time, but later his grandpa said that he knew who Jason was right away.

Susan was very happy to have found the son she had lost, and she and Jason met. It wasn't long before Jason wanted Susan to meet his adoptive parents and to come to his wedding. This was too difficult for Susan, and she chose not to come to the wedding. She had wanted to raise this child. It took years, but finally it was Susan who initiated contact with Jason's adoptive parents. This came at about the time Josh, Jason's oldest boy, was born. Grandchildren can warm grandparents' hearts in a way nothing else can. A little over a year later, Susan was rewarded with twin grandsons.

It took Susan ten years, but now she can talk with those who raised Jason and can see her grandchildren. Now Jason attends reunions with his birth mother and half sister Miranda. They see each other every year. At this particular time, Jason is headed to Florida to spend four days with his birth family.

Heidi watched the relationships grow between Jason and his birth family. She felt that it was good. But it did not cause her to look for her own birth family. She had a great family with Jason and her adoptive parents.

At Heidi and Jason's family reunion about five years ago, Susan said to Jason's adoptive parents how thankful she was for what they had done for Jason. Susan knew she couldn't have provided what they had provided for Jason during his growing-up years. This cemented the relationship between the two sets of parents and opened up a new understanding and appreciation of what these adoptive parents had provided over the years. They had wanted children and had provided everything to this girl and boy that they would have provided to children born to them. They'd had no part in the situations that had brought these children to them, and they had provided the love and stable family that these two had needed at that time.

Todd Stark fell in love with Heidi. Knowing the wonderful person she was, he wanted to meet her birth mother. He was so curious that he dug through the Internet but wasn't able to find anything. He knew Heidi's mom's name, as it was on her original birth certificate.

Heidi told him the story about the time she and her adoptive mother had driven through Hershey, Nebraska, when she was a teenager. Heidi told her mom that she thought she was from Hershey because she liked chocolate so much. The name Hershey is the same as that of Hershey, Pennsylvania, where the famous chocolate factory is located. Heidi's adoptive mother said that it actually was true. Heidi was from Hershey, Nebraska.

With this information, Todd became more active in trying to find Heidi's family. Heidi was no help, but if you knew her, you would understand why. She graduated from dental school and became a pediatric dentist. Soon she opened her own practice and then expanded it by building a brand new office in another part of town. All this was happening while she started her family. She has Augie, a four-year-old boy, and Elizabeth, a three-year-old girl. There weren't too many free minutes in her day. When you add in the fact that she was a Division I University of Nebraska team golfer—who still holds a handicap index of 1.9 at the Lincoln Country Club—you begin to realize the caliber of this person.

Todd continued his search and found a friend at their church who was from the Hershey, Nebraska, area. This friend, Dick Clark, was about seventy years old, and he said he would search around Hershey to see if he could find Heidi's birth mother. Soon after that, he came to church with two photos from an old high school annual. It was from the years when Heidi's mother would have been in school. The girls in the photos had Heidi's birth mother's maiden name and were named Mary and JoAnn.

Todd told Heidi's adoptive mother that they had two photos of girls who must have been cousins of Heidi's birth mother, Amanda. Heidi's adoptive mother corrected Todd, saying that Heidi's birth mother was Amelia not Amanda. Now they were getting close. As soon as they returned home, Todd started searching on Facebook by putting the name Amelia in the search box. He found an Amelia Mary. He told Heidi that this could be her birth mom. He crafted a message to her privately on Facebook. This was June of the year that Augie, Heidi's oldest child, was about nine months old. Seeing the wonders and miracles of her own child, Heidi began to realize how hard it would be to give up one's child. She began to feel that it was important to meet her birth mother, if that was possible.

In 2007 Heidi's birth mother's husband, Terry, said to his wife, after thirty years of marriage, that someone could come knocking at their door, and it might be the daughter she'd given away. Mary answered him, "I don't think so. It has been about thirty-four years now. Some accident could have happened, and she might not even be alive now." Mary and Terry basically never talked about this daughter. Mary was very closemouthed about her experience, and Terry didn't know if she wanted to talk about this first baby. Terry had been supportive of Mary finding her daughter from the day she'd told him about her when they were dating, but Mary had shoved this conversation out of her mind. Still, deep inside, she had always wondered where Heidi might be, what she was doing, and where she lived. She felt she had given up her right to have any connection with this daughter.

One time, Mary saw the mother of her youngest daughter's friend when the girls were twelve years old. She thought that this mother was young enough to be her daughter. In reality, the mother was probably about Heidi's age. Mary actually said to the lady, "You are young enough to be my daughter." These things haunted Mary so much that she put her feelings in a box and closed the lid. This helped somewhat, but sometimes thoughts inside her screamed of a thirty-four-year-old daughter. Mary says that she put a stone wall around her heart so no one could get in. It was easier not to feel at all.

One Christmas, Baylee, Mary's daughter, asked for the movie *Juno* as her gift. This is a story about a pregnant teen who intended to abort her baby, changed her mind, carried the baby to term, and then released her to adoptive parents. Mary was able to watch *Juno* with Baylee without shedding a tear. Mary does remember the film well, as she said there were protestors outside the abortion clinic, saying, "Your baby has fingernails." But Mary didn't cry. The box now had a stone wall around it.

One day in 2009, Baylee, now a senior in high school, said to Mary, "Mom, you should have a Facebook account. Mary didn't want one. She was busy being the class president's mother and attending meetings for the prom and graduation parties for the end of the year. She didn't have time to mess with Facebook. She liked mowing the lawn, being outside, and watching Baylee play volleyball. Baylee set up an account for Mary as a joke, putting in her birth date as 1905. A couple of months after having Facebook, which Mary didn't use, she decided that someone from her former home in the southwest might try to look her up by her maiden name. She added her maiden name to the account. Little did she know who else knew her maiden name. But God knew, and He also knew that something very special was going to happen to Mary. Perhaps He coaxed her to add her maiden name to the Facebook account.

Nolan, Mary's oldest son, was a teacher, and sometimes Mary helped him with his papers at her house. Quite often, he got on her computer and showed her Christian videos. One day in May of 2010—only about six weeks before Mary knew that Heidi's husband was looking for her—Nolan showed Mary two wonderful music videos on YouTube. They were written and sung by an adopted adult named Mark Schultz.

Mark realized one day that his mother had had three choices when she became pregnant with him. She could have an abortion; she could give him birth and keep him, not caring about the fact that she was very poor and had no way to care for him; or she could do the most unselfish thing and love him so much that she would give him life and then find him loving parents who had much to offer him. Before this realization of his birth mother's unselfishness, Mark hadn't been much interested in her, because she had given him away. Now he understood what she had given him. So he sat down and wrote "Everything to Me," sang it, and placed the video on YouTube. In the year 2014, this video was still playing on YouTube. It contains these words and more:

> I must have felt your tears,
> I must have heard you say goodbye,
> You gave me a brand new world
> So I could play baseball in the yard.
> You gave me everything.
> Thank you.

This video was later passed on to Heidi and Jason, which helped them understand the emotions that had made Mary put up her stone wall.

The second video stated that a pregnant mother had heard these words as she was planning an abortion. She cancelled her appointment and chose adoption for her child. This child was saved because Mark Schultz had sung this song and put it on YouTube. Mary didn't listen to the video very long. She wondered why Nolan was showing it to her. He couldn't possibly know her deeply buried secret.

Another time, Nolan logged Mary in on Facebook and told her to send a message to a friend. Mary rarely got on Facebook herself, and she certainly didn't know that she could get a private message. Nolan saw the message from Todd Stark, who was looking for a birth mom by the name of Mary. Nolan asked Mary if he could tell Todd that he had the wrong person, as the person Todd was looking for obviously wasn't the Mary he knew. Mary was his mother. She had five children and had never mentioned another child. Mary told Nolan that she would take care of the message. Mary did not know then that soon her life would be changed forever.

Mary kept that message in her mind and responded to it at a later time. Mary learned a lot about Facebook by herself. She gave Todd her e-mail address and said, "Let's communicate." She even changed her password. That was the easy part. Now she had to share this message with her whole family, and she had no idea where to start. Later, Nolan asked Mary, in front of her husband, Terry, "Mom, did you tell those people they had the wrong person?"

"Yes," Mary said. She had gotten very good at lying and hiding after thirty-six years. Now she couldn't even sleep. She knew she had to come clean, so she started with Nolan. It then took her four days to tell Terry that the message had been from her daughter—just as he had suspected earlier. Why was this so hard for her to do? He had known her secret since before they were married. But Mary couldn't tell him, so she printed off the message and gave it to him.

The note from Todd Stark was very discreet:

> You may know my wife from November 3rd of 1973 in Lincoln, NE. Her birth mother's name was Amelia, and she was about eighteen years old. I am hoping that you may be this person.
>
> If you are her birth mother, I apologize for the intrusion into your life. I understand that you may want to keep this private. My wife, Heidi, and I recently had our son, and it became very clear to her and to me that the blessing of our son would not be possible without her birth mother deciding to have Heidi. "Thank you" does not express how grateful we are to you and to God for blessing us with her life. Heidi and our family have

been praying for you for many years. We hope all is well and that you have been blessed beyond anything we could ever hope for.

May God bless you and give you peace to know that you have made an incredible impact on our lives.

Sincerely,
Todd Stark

Amelia Mary replied at 1:00 a.m. on 6/25/10: "Wow! Yes, I am this person. I have always wondered if this would ever happen. Yes, I would like to keep this private. Very few people in my life know about this. I actually am not a Facebook person! My daughter made me an account about a year ago, and I never use it. So I have no idea what is private and what is not. At this time, I would rather you contact me by e-mail."

Todd responded by giving Mary both his and Heidi's phone numbers and e-mail addresses. Mary kept checking her e-mail every day, but nothing was there. Finally, on 7/1/10 at 12:22 a.m., she checked her junk mail and was so excited to see the response hiding there. They set an approximate time to meet, and Mary told Todd about Heidi's five siblings. Mary wrote, "Maybe tonight I can get some sleep!"

Heidi wasn't home when Todd got the e-mail that her birth mother was coming at 10:30 p.m. that night to meet her. Heidi came home exhausted, as she had won two matches in the state golf tournament that day, matches that she hadn't been expected to win. She could hardly believe it when Todd said, "Your birth mother is coming to meet you at 10:30 tonight." Heidi wanted to be fresh and ready to meet this person whom she had heard looked like her. Her physician, Dr. Fletcher, had been at the adoption process and had mentioned to her one time that she sure looked like her birth mother. What excitement entered Heidi's chest at that time! It had already been a great day, and now she was going to meet her birth mother that same evening.

Mary's husband and son arrived at Heidi and Todd's home before Mary did, sometime between 10:30 and 11:00 p.m. The excitement began even before Mary got there in a different car. Heidi opened the front door as soon as Mary arrived in the driveway. Heidi watched her walk up the sidewalk to their front door and was amazed that she could finally meet her birth mother. They talked and talked. Heidi learned about her half siblings:

- Nolan, a teacher
- Landon, a nurse practitioner and chiropractor
- Curtis, a college grad wanting to be a dentist
- Logan, in medical school
- Baylee, headed to dental school

Yes, four out of five of her half siblings, not knowing her at all, had chosen medical fields just as she had, and two of them wanted to specialize in dentistry! Now Heidi knew that she had another family and that they were very much like her. She was been welcomed by all and has been invited to participate in family weddings and more.

Heidi's birth mother loved her own mother so much that she had never told her about the pregnancy in which she carried Heidi. She had not wanted to let her mom down. The only people in the family who had known about Heidi's birth were Mary's husband and her aunt and uncle who lived in the Sandhills of Nebraska. Mary had gone to them because they had adopted a son through Lutheran Family Services, and they would know what to do. This aunt and uncle, Jim and Dotty, helped Mary to go to Lincoln, Nebraska, live in a private home, and provide a family for her baby. They visited the state fair before dropping Mary off at the private home. Mary had never again attended the fair because of her memories.

Mary remembered living with a family and helping take care of their daughter Liisa. One night after Heidi had met her birth mother, she and Todd were talking in bed, and Todd said, "I know a Liisa who spells her name that way." He placed a text to Liisa's family and asked if they had provided a home for pregnant women at one time. The answer was yes. This meant that Todd and Heidi had been only two blocks from each other at the time Todd was born.

It is a miracle that these two women were reunited. They discovered times when other family members had been in close contact with each other, but different circumstances finally brought them together. It was a special gift from God that things happened the way they did. Mary told Heidi that she had grieved for her for thirty-seven years. The second night that Mary and Heidi talked, Heidi asked her if it was hard on Heidi's birthdays. Mary answered, "Not a day went by that I didn't think about you."

The reunion happened at a very hard time for Mary. Her youngest daughter was going away to college. She had homeschooled each of her children for a time and was feeling a great loss. This feeling was exasperated by finding Heidi and remembering afresh her great loss when she had placed Heidi for adoption. Heidi tells her now, "You did the right thing; you gave to me what Christ gives us. You gave me life, and He gives eternal life. How wonderful is that?"

When Mary met Heidi's adoptive mom, she wasn't ready. She was so emotional, she couldn't even talk. The thirty-seven years were hard, but now when Mary comes to Heidi's home, she and her husband are Grandma and Grandpa to Heidi and Todd's children. Heidi also told her birth mom, "I had a wonderful life, and my adoptive parents raised me well, but I am not perfect. I caused some troubles. You need to talk to my mom to understand some of the things I did as a child."

Mary said to Todd and Heidi, "It has been two months today that I stumbled onto your message that turned my life upside down. Actually it was already upside down, and your message made it right side up."

Turning to You

This reunion of children and birth moms is a wonderful miracle that brings joy to all. When Heidi refers to the eternal life Jesus gives, she is referring to a Bible verse in John 5:24: "I tell you the truth, whoever hears my word and believes him who sent me has eternal life and will not be condemned; he has crossed over from death to life." Christ died for us and is preparing a home in heaven for His followers. You can have this eternal life also by accepting Jesus into your heart and being sorry for any wrong things you have done.

Prayer

Our Father in heaven, thank You for the life given to Heidi and Jason. These two were brought up to know You. They were well educated and are giving back to their communities and families in a grand way. Thank You, Lord, for being "able to do immeasurably more than all we ask or imagine" (Ephesians 3:20a). Amen.

8

Two Ways to Get Kids and Love Them Both

DeLoris Tonack

DeLoris and her husband, Tom, were both teachers and were ready to have a baby. But it just didn't happen. Adoption was an easy choice because Tom had been adopted and had come to know that he was a very lucky boy. They contacted Lutheran Family Services in Omaha, Nebraska, in 1970 for an application to adopt a child. They proceeded through all the interviews and had a caseworker visit them at home. They knew this visit was to check out their home living situation, and they believed it was a good idea. After all, adopting a child was a very special privilege, and they wanted to be open and show that they could raise and love a child.

After hearing stories of people waiting to hear back from the agency for long periods of time, they proceeded with their teaching. Very soon, Tom received a call at school on April 13. The voice on the other end said, "We have a baby for you, born today, which you can pick up next Tuesday." He was flabbergasted and tried to think how he, the husband, would tell DeLoris, the wife, that they were going to have a baby. He contemplated that fact all day and kept quiet to everyone else in the building, which is a very difficult thing to do when you have just become a father. On the way out the door, he couldn't help himself, and he told one other person that he and DeLoris were getting a baby the following week.

It happened that the one person Tom told about the call lived across the street from where DeLoris was getting her hair cut. As she came out the door, this teacher saw DeLoris and, knowing her from school, said, "Congratulations on the baby." Of course, she was anxious to be one of the first to say those words to DeLoris. But DeLoris said, "Do we have a baby?" The look on the teacher's face told the story. "Oh my goodness, you don't know?" she said, covering her mouth in horror.

DeLoris entered her house, throwing the door open wide and letting the cold air flow in. She shouted, "We are getting a baby?" Tom answered, "Who told you?" Needless to say, they were both so excited that no one was blamed for the news being spread as it was.

The next day, funny as it may seem, DeLoris was giving a baby shower for another teacher at the school. She was able to say, "We are getting a baby too." It was a wonderful day for her. She spent the afternoon calling friends and relatives with the news. It wasn't easy, as she kept dialing the wrong numbers. Her fingers weren't working well because of the excitement she felt. She and Tom were on top of the world. They were going to be a family!

Since this was in the 70s, they put their little boy, whom they named Mark, into a basket in the car. There were no baby car seats in those days. They drove miles to go to Tom's parents' home to show them the child. In their excitement, they had neglected to call ahead, and no one was home. So they headed home with their little baby boy.

Nothing could dampen their happiness, not even the fact that their jobs provided no maternity or paternity leave. They had this one-week-old baby and were expected to show up for work the rest of the week. They took Wednesday off and tried to get their ducks in a row. They decided that DeLoris would have to take a dock in pay and take Thursday and Friday off too.

What would they do for baby clothes, and how would they care for Mark while they were teaching? The reality of it all started to sink in. There were six weeks of school left on their contracts. The next-door neighbor must have been sent by an angel because she brought clothes for the baby and agreed to care for him for the rest of the school year while Tom and DeLoris were working.

The adoption was closed, and everything was secret. They completed the adoption after the six-month waiting period. DeLoris caught a glimpse of the mother's last name, which ended with the letters -*son*. In the Swedish community around Kearney, Nebraska, it didn't matter much, because there were so many Petersons, Johnsons, Andersons, Carlsons, and other -sons that DeLoris did not know who the mother was. However, she tucked that little bit of information into her heart, as that was the name of her son's biological mother. About two years later, she saw a bridal announcement of a lady who had the same last name she thought she had seen before. If this bride was her son's mother, then she now also knew the mother's married name. All this remained in the back of DeLoris's mind.

The big shock came when DeLoris realized that she was pregnant. Now she was in Tom's shoes and could tell him about their second baby coming within a year. The two children were ten and a half months apart. Tom and DeLoris experienced both ways to get kids.

Being familiar with adoption, and knowing Tom's love for his adoptive parents, these two teachers found it very easy to love both children equally. They understood that both children accepted their love. In fact, when DeLoris found out that their adopted son, Mark, wanted to follow the policy of the Lutheran Family Service and request the name of his parents at age twenty-five, DeLoris hoped and prayed that the mother had left a letter saying she would like to meet her son. DeLoris wanted Mark to know his biological mother because it was something he wanted, and it would be good to find out that she loved him.

When Mark got a letter from a lady in their town saying that she was his mother, DeLoris recognized the name. She told Mark that she and Tom were okay with him meeting her. Because DeLoris loved Mark so much, she said that bringing his biological mother to meet them would have to be his choice. Mark chose to have his birth mother meet his adoptive parents, and DeLoris found out that she had been right about the -*son* person all along. Mark was able to meet his step siblings, but he never heard from his birth father. The relationship was good, but the meetings soon ended. Mark is satisfied with his situation of having one close family where he knows he is loved immensely and equally with his sibling.

Turning to You

"The creation of humanity was an act of sheer uncalled for extravagance, wholly unnecessary. That is just the way the Lord is, doing nothing out of personal need but only out of His own abundantly overflowing life" (Mike, Mason, *The Gospel According to Job*).

DeLoris and Tom experienced a wonderful understanding of the creation of human life when they found out that they were going to adopt a baby. They were exhilarated and delighted to receive the special gift of a child through adoption. Then they had a child by natural birth, which was a blessing only God could have presented to them.

"There's no such thing as adopted children. There are only children who were adopted. In a biblical understanding, 'adopted' is a past-tense verb, not an adjective. So once someone has been adopted into the family, that person is part of the family with everything that that means" (Russell Moore, dean of the School of Theology at Southern Baptist Theological Seminary).

Prayer

We appreciate You, Lord, just the way You are, creating life and giving us joy. Thank You for blessing DeLoris and Tom. Amen.

Reason 3

God Prepares Families for Children

9

Unselfish Behavior Shows Love

Kristie and Joey Holmberg

Kristie and Joey had no children, and they were sitting around one night in February of 2001, enjoying the evening. The phone rang. "Would you take temporary custody of three children? Their mother has been arrested, and we were told to call you." In the conversation, they found out that Kristie's sister was the one who had been arrested, and these children were their relatives. They looked at each other and said, "We can try it." For one whole week, they had no clue where the children were. Kristie and Joey were checked out by officials to see if their home qualified for placement of children.

About a week later, Kristie and Joey had three children, ages three, four, and seven, all sleeping in the same bedroom in their two-bedroom condo. They had to sign the children up for school and set up a day care schedule. The children were considered wards of the state, thank goodness. The Department of Human Services provided some monetary help and health insurance.

The children's mother was given time to get her life straightened out, and she got them back for a while, but it wasn't long before

Kristie and Joey had the children back in their lives. This was a big adjustment, as they had become set in their ways, both were working, and they were used to having the weekends and evenings to themselves.

Within three months' time, they changed jobs, bought a house, and took in the three children. Joey had been in his job for sixteen years. The couple learned to accept the change in their lifestyle. Now they are both proud to say that the kids have been in the same school for thirteen years. The oldest boy had been in five schools during his kindergarten and first-grade years. One of Joey's most vivid memories was of taking Bobby to Clive School on the first day they had him. They arrived in front of the school fifteen minutes early, so Joey asked Bobby if he wanted to sit in the car for a while. "No, that's okay," Bobby said, and he walked right into the middle of the group of strangers that were his new classmates.

At this point, Joey realized that Bobby was a tough little boy who could live in the moment and put his past behind him. He and Kristie could give these three children love and consistency. Richard L. Strauss wrote in *The Joy of Knowing God* that "God is love and one of our greatest needs as human beings is to be loved. We all need love. We need to know that we are important to somebody, that somebody truly cares about us, wants us, and accepts us unconditionally. When we doubt that we are loved, we may develop unacceptable behavior patterns to compensate for it." Kristie and Joey wanted to be the parents who proved to these three children that somebody truly cared. He and Kristie could provide the love Bobby, Sonny, and Megan needed for the rest of their lives.

Besides keeping the children in the same school for years, Kristie and Joey have been able to keep Bobby, Sonny, and Megan together. The couple realized that being together has been the constant in the children's lives. Two and a half years after Kristie and Joey started caring for the children, the birth parents' rights were terminated by the courts. Today, Sonny, the youngest, is a sophomore in high school, Megan is graduating from high school, and Bobby is in the United States Army.

Joey talks proudly of his son Bobby. This father, who had no children, changed his life to father three children. He knows it is because of his and his wife's home that Bobby was able to be involved in wrestling and baseball. All of the trips to the gyms and fields were worth it. Their town of Norwalk, Iowa, was the smallest in the largest wrestling class in Iowa. Bobby had a record of twenty-four wins and twelve losses. An award named after the school's longtime wrestling coach, which is given to only one wrestler a year, was presented to Bobby. It is given to someone who has fought adversity and stuck it out.

Joey tells about this shining moment in Bobby's career. They were wrestling their school rival and were down by five points. Bobby was the last wrestler, and the only way the team could win was for Bobby to get a pin. Bobby pinned his opponent in one and a half minutes. The team didn't have to wait long to see that Bobby had the stuff needed to bring home the win. These are the things that make a father proud.

Bobby continues to make Kristie and Joey proud. When he left for the US Army, he signed up to work on Apache helicopters. Now he has put in a request to be in the Army Special Forces, which is the US Army's division equal to the US Navy Seals. Joey understands the dangers, but he knows that Bobby will serve his God and country well.

Sonny, the youngest, is also involved in football and wrestling at Norwalk school. Sonny has aspirations of going into the army to serve our country like his big brother did. The one thing Joey believes will hold Sonny back a little is that he hasn't learned to take orders as well as Bobby. This might come with time.

Megan, the middle child, is very social and makes friends wherever she goes. Megan shows a remarkable capability for handling and caring for children. Being an aunt to Kristie's oldest sister's children is one of her joys. It is regularly said that Megan is their favorite aunt. Joey knows this talent will serve her well as she goes through her life, cares for little ones, and helps others.

Joey's first job as a photography studio representative caused him to travel to various cities such as Wichita, Kansas; Indianapolis, Indiana; Omaha, Nebraska; and Las Vegas, Nevada, When he left this job, he did not know how he would provide for the children. He just knew that he was needed at home to help Kristie. He started work in the mortgage business, which has few set hours and very little guaranteed pay. Kristie took six months leave from Century Link Company to help the kids adjust. Their home life and their careers were interrupted by the adoption of these children. They are thankful to have some monetary help for each child until each reaches the age of eighteen.

The sacrifices of Kristie and Joey have provided a normal life for these kids. Kristie's mother and Joey's parents have been very helpful and caring grandparents, and they came to help when Kristie and Joey needed assistance. They have loaded the kids up and taken trips across the country with extended family members, and they love family time together. This family had been ill prepared *emotionally* and *financially* when the children arrived. But the changes Kristie and Joey made in their lives in order to parent Bobby, Megan, and Sonny, clearly demonstrate that God had prepared this family *mentally* and *spiritually* for the job—long before Kristie and Joey knew what was going to happen. "'For I know the plans I have for you,' declares the Lord, 'plans to prosper you and not to harm you, plans to give you hope and a future'" (Jeremiah 29:11).

Jesus loved the little children and said in Matthew 19:14: "Let the little children come to me; and do not hinder them, for the Kingdom of heaven belongs to such as these."

Turning to You

God can prepare us for anything. Think of a time when you thought you could not possibly make it through something that happened to you. Did you have enough faith to act in the way Kristie and Joey did when a ready-made family was dropped into their home? "We are not in the family we are in by chance. God is sovereign and has placed us where he wants us to be for his glory and the building of his kingdom" (Don Fields, *LifeGuide Bible Study: Nehemiah*, Lesson 7).

Prayer

Thank You, Lord, for being with Kristie and Joey as they parented these three children of Yours. It is a miracle that You know ahead of time and prepare those You want to care for Your little ones. May You continue to be with Bobby, Megan, and Sonny as they serve our country and care for others as they have been cared for in their adoptive home. Thank You, Lord, that Kristie and Joey did as You said in Psalm 119:36: "Turn my heart toward your statutes and not toward selfish gain." In Jesus' name, amen.

10

God Prepared the Way for Love

Craig and Linda Eley

Linda had always wanted to be a mommy. She was raised with religion. Then she met Craig. He had a story to tell her that changed her understanding of religion. He explained that many people are walking around with an emptiness, trying to fill it with all sorts of things. Linda knew she was missing something, and Craig led her to understand that God created us to need Him. Craig also told her that God wants a relationship with us and that Jesus died so that our sins are forgiven. This information was something new to Linda, but she felt that a lightbulb had just lit up her life. She married Craig six months later. All she wanted then was to have kids, be a stay-at-home mom, and teach her children about God's love.

Her dream came true. The couple had lean years and lived in the country with their little family of three children. Craig started a family business, and they moved to Lincoln. Before they knew it, Brian, their youngest child, was eleven years old. "But … but," she said, "I am not done being a mom." She thought about volunteering at a hospital to help with the babies. Many other thoughts also came into her head. But nothing seemed to fulfill her desire to parent more children.

Then one day Craig sat at the dining table with the five Eleys and said, "Somebody is missing." They all looked at each other. No one was missing. The truth was that none of the existing family was missing. After much discussion, Linda realized that Craig had a desire for more children too. It didn't take them long to come to the conclusion that they both wanted to adopt. They looked into domestic and international adoptions. The churches they were familiar with had stopped financing international adoptions. The domestic adoptions were more expensive than they could afford. They had one income and three children to educate. What could they do?

They decided to sign up for foster care training, to wait and see what would happen. Linda believed that waiting for what she wanted helped her to wait on God. If God wanted them to have more children, He would make it possible. She waited. After a year, a call came, asking if they could take in twins who needed medical help. They knew they couldn't take the twins for the long term, and they were glad when they heard that a family had adopted the children.

By this time, the Eleys' daughter had received a scholarship to play volleyball at the University of Wyoming. Life became more complicated. Six months later, they got a call to accept a week-old little girl. They were asked to be an adoptive home for her. However, the adoption fell through because of complications involving a couple in California who were relatives of the little girl. There were rumors of meth use by the mother. Linda continued to believe that they were supposed to have this little girl. And she was right. The authorities brought Paige to the Eleys when she was three weeks old. The mother had decided she wanted her baby back, but the state had determined that she wasn't capable of raising the child because of her addiction.

Two years later, after they had fallen in love with little Paige, the mother was granted a visit with the child. Linda and Craig realized that they had to surrender Paige's situation to God, no matter how painful it would be if she did not return home to them. After praying, they were freed from anxiety and decided to accept whatever was decided for Paige's future. And Paige did come home to them. The older children joined Linda and Craig in celebration. The family had accepted Paige as one of them. The love between Craig, Linda, the older siblings, and little Paige felt like a cup overflowing.

The waiting wasn't over, even when the parental rights were terminated. Paige was three years old before they could actually adopt her. They realized how thankful they were that Paige was now legally a part of the Eley family. Craig remembered that he'd had visions of Linda shortly after receiving Christ into his life. He didn't actually meet her until two years later. In the same way, it seemed to him that God was already preparing them to have additional family.

Linda was delighted to know that Paige would grow up in their home. It was great being an older mom. She was more patient. It was evident to her that problems like being up all night, potty training, and other difficult stages were short-lived. She was more content to be tied down with a little one in the house than she'd been when she was a young and inexperienced mom. It was a great learning experience for the older children to have a smaller dependent child around the house. The age difference was great; their daughter, Samantha, graduated when Paige was six months old, and she continues to live in Wyoming. The foster care group Craig and Linda were in was magnificent and helped them through tough times. Craig and Linda had gone through extensive training and joined a support group, had wanted Paige very badly, and were now older and wiser, so just imagine the care and love this little girl received. Add to that the adoration of the three older children for Paige.

"What are you thinking of?" Linda's mother said to her. "You are dreaming of another child?"

"Yes," said Linda, "and it is a curly-headed toddler."

"I am not sure you can do this anymore," said her mother.

Well, the call came. Paige's birth mother had had another little girl named Piper. Linda had heard that sometimes mothers who have to give up a child often replace that child with a new baby. Piper had been born, and her mother had kept her until she was twenty-one months old. Parental rights had been terminated again, and this baby was available for adoption. Craig and Linda knew it was Paige's little sister. How could they refuse to let these two little girls grow up together? Piper looked like the little child Linda had seen in her dream.

Some problems arrived with little Piper. She had already become attached to her biological mother and her grandmother. This was different from Paige's situation, as Paige had been only three weeks old. Piper upset Paige because she cried every day for two weeks. Paige said, "Mommy, please send her back." The crying caused family stress, and times were difficult for about six months. It took all those months before Linda could say to Piper, "I love you with my whole heart." Having waited until she felt the unconditional love, Linda knew the love was real.

Another difficulty the Eleys suffered was in going to court when the grandparents tried to legally obtain custody of little Piper. Not only was it difficult to make the court dates each time, but it was an emotional struggle. They prayed that the decision the judge made would be the best for the little girl. It was not their desire to remove Piper from her grandparents if it was God's will for her to be with them. But they were well aware that they would be able to keep the two sisters together.

The waiting went on and on. They had Piper in their home, but they had no security that she would stay there. The little curly-headed toddler was warming up to them, but the grieving process had taken a toll on her too. At the end of the day, all of them felt like they had climbed a mountain. They decided to give Piper the middle name of Grace. Because of their struggles, this verse in 2 Corinthians 9:8 is very meaningful to the Eleys. "And God is able to make all grace abound to you, so that in all things at all times, having all that you need, you will abound in every good work." They received all they needed, including the knowledge that God's will was done in their process of adopting Paige and Piper.

Turning to You

Linda wanted to be a mommy, and Craig felt that someone was still missing from their family dinner table, even when all the members were there. Linda saw visions of a little curly-headed girl. Who do you suppose highlighted those thoughts in their heads? God was aware that Paige and Piper were going to need a home, and He knew exactly when they would need it. Linda and Craig were ready at the right time to take them into their family. God is observing us all the time. Job 7:20 refers to God as the "watcher of men." Did God make Linda and Craig aware that these little ones needed parents, preparing them to love the girls? We must think that He did, considering His words to Job: "Who endowed the heart with wisdom or gave understanding to the mind?" (Job 38:36).

Prayer

Thank You, Lord, for opening up homes for little ones who need moms and dads. Please continue to give Linda and Craig the support they need to raise the girls, and hear their prayers for their family. Thank You that Jesus taught us His command: "Love each other as I have loved you" (John 15:12). Amen.

11

The Girls Needed Her, and Her Purpose Was to Love

Angela Pillow

Having been raised by her mother along with three sisters and a brother in Mobile, Alabama, and having been taught that each person has a purpose in life, Angela knew what to do. She was twenty-four years old and was attending a "Safe Night" that she had organized for the Big Brothers and Big Sisters organization through Americorps, whose desire was to keep kids away from drugs. Angela's four-year-old daughter, who was with her, came running in fear, yelling, "He hit me!" She pointed to a child close by. Angela saw that the child seemed to be a girl, not a boy. Angela put the two young girls together and said, "Let's start over. Let's be friends." She had them exchange names amidst the noise of the break dancers.

Another day, Angela saw the same little girl in her neighborhood and realized that she and her three siblings were neighbors. They became friends. Seeing that the little girl from Safe Night was not receiving guidance from her mother, Angela wanted to become a Big

Sister to the family. This was impossible because the waiting period was very long. Angela noticed that this little girl and her siblings not only needed guidance but that they were beautiful, smart, and very talented. The girls could sing very well, and Justin, the boy, was a terrific dancer. Angela realized that God must have brought this family to her for a reason. They invited her to go to church with them. She came to believe the gospel and to know Jesus as her Savior. With this knowledge, she concluded that she would just become the children's Big Sister outside of the organization, and she would start immediately. Her prayers were for the Lord to take her and use her.

Over many years, Angela was available to all four siblings in this family. They confided to Angela that she had been the guiding light in their lives, and the reason they didn't work in the strip club or pursue other bad habits. The oldest girl had a daughter named Adrianna, who was precious to Angela, like a granddaughter. But it happened that the state took Adrianna away from her mother because of an incident. Angela applied to be her foster parent, but she wasn't approved in time to have Adrianna placed in her home. In the foster home where Adrianna was placed, she was sexually abused by an older girl and was removed. Finally, Adrianna became Angela's foster daughter. Today, Adrianna is doing well in second grade and has achieved third-grade reading and math levels.

Angela applied to adopt Adrianna, as she had become just like her own child. A date was set for the adoption, but Adrianna's birth father came into the picture. He had not been involved in her life over the first eight years. He applied for custody of Adrianna, even though Adrianna had only met him once. The court terminated his rights, but he has appealed that decision. He continues to call and talk to Adrianna on the phone.

This adoption has not gone through at this writing, but it is easy to see the love among Angela and the four siblings who invited her to their church. Their relationship has given guidance to the siblings and has brought Adrianna to Angela's home, an arrangement that will hopefully become permanent soon.

Turning to You

This is an example of one of the various ways that children become loved by those who are not their biological parents. You can be part of an uplifting story by being willing to guide, love, and raise children who were not born to you.

Prayer

Help us listen to You, Lord. Bring us to repentance so we can follow You. "Now that you have purified yourselves by obeying the truth so that you have sincere love for your brothers, love one another deeply, from the heart" (1 Peter 1:22). Lead us to love deeply from the heart like Angela. Amen.

12

The Child They Were Supposed to Love

Larry and Melody Lennox

Larry and Melody Lennox looked at the proof of their infertility. They had tried medical options, and nothing had been successful. They wanted children. Things were changing in the adoption world. People were doing open adoptions, which allowed the baby to know all birth parents and their families. The Lennoxes weren't sure that was for them.

They proceeded to pursue a private adoption in the old-fashioned way, and they adopted Megan at two days old. They knew very little about her parents, and this plan worked for them. Life changed when they brought their little girl home, and it was wonderful. They wanted more children and siblings for Megan. They realized that it didn't matter if the child looked like the parents, the way one's biological children might. The joy was in raising a little child in one's home. The joy was in being a family. Larry explained that they began to realize that Megan was the child they were supposed to have and love. It seemed as though this union had been decided a long time ago. It just felt so right.

Megan had been born in Kansas, and they checked into adopting another child in the same way they had adopted Megan. They realized that domestic adoptions were becoming more difficult, took more time, and were more apt to be in the open style. They felt a desire to look at foreign adoptions. They were led to proceed in that manner for their second and third children. In 2002 Larry and Melody were still within the age limit for Chinese adoptions. However, they discovered after the bombing of the Twin Towers in New York City that procedures were more controlled by Homeland Security. They had to be fingerprinted and go through a lot of paperwork, but they had faith that the system would produce a positive result.

In China the disease called SARS (Severe Acute Respiratory Syndrome) was raging. They had to wait awhile, but they were in the first group allowed to proceed after babies were available for adoption again. The parents left Megan with neighbors and went to get Sidney, who was in a small, southern Chinese town that was fairly prosperous. They found that the Chinese had the procedure down, and the adoption was quick. Holt International (a trusted leader in international adoptions for over fifty years) used trains that arrived on time. Larry and Melody spent two weeks in the country as they traveled to the city where their adoption was to be processed. They started in Beijing, which was prosperous to the degree that not many adoptions occurred there. In Beijing the Lennoxes felt that they were on vacation and sightseeing, as the weather was beautiful.

Adoption officials told the Lennoxes that the first person who takes the baby in the handoff is soon rejected by the baby because the baby feels that this person has taken it away from what it knows. The Chinese representatives were helpful to Larry and Melody because Larry took the handoff, and then Sidney wanted to be with Melody. This made Melody extremely happy. The advice proved to be true.

As they were strolling with the baby in a nice area around the hotel, they noticed a lot of martial arts people around. These extremely fit people and others would stop Larry and Melody when they noticed foreigners with a Chinese baby. Thankfully, the Lennoxes had an official card with them that explained that they were adopting according to government order. The best part was when the Chinese then said to Larry and Melody, "Lucky baby." When they conversed with an older Chinese person, they felt the admiration because of the alliance between China and America in World War II. One Chinese person they met explained this to the Lennoxes.

A high point of their visit to China was when Larry, Melody, and Sidney saw the panda in the zoo. Sidney was only eleven months old, and she was wide-eyed as they passed by the animals. Soon the consulate processed their papers, and they were off to the airport for the trip home. This wasn't as easy as they had hoped, because the plane had some trouble and was diverted to another airport. In the states, we tend to take this type of delay with a fair amount of ease, but it is not so in a foreign country so far from home. The Lennoxes wondered about the safety regulations.

Their excitement was so great that Larry left their documents, which they sorely needed at the Domestic Security gate, on the plane at one stop. They ran back to get them and barely made it back on the next plane. Things were calmer after they arrived in the United States, and they headed over to retrieve Megan from their friends. After finally arriving home with their new little girl and Megan, they were so tired and stressed from all the travel, adoption activity, and plane shenanigans, that they actually lost memory of the last few hours.

Again the Lennoxes began to realize that they wanted to expand their family further. This time it didn't take nearly ten years as it had between the first two adoptions. They proceeded to adopt Paula, who was only two years younger than Sidney. This time they decided to take Megan and Sidney with them to China. On Christmas Eve, they arrived at the Great Wall of China on a very cold night. The guides assigned to Larry and Melody were competent, but the province where they picked up eight-month-old Paula was very poor. Many times they experienced rolling blackouts. In spite of the complications at this extremely poor place, many adoptions were processed in the area.

Paula became sick with flu-like symptoms on the trip, and Larry had to take her to a hospital in China. The hospital reminded him of his own hometown clinic back in 1953. The x-ray machine was old, but the cost was only five dollars. Soon afterward, Paula became better, but the rest of the family caught the bug as they traveled home. There were no plans for help when they arrived in Omaha, and the way Larry and Melody felt, there was no way they could drive home with the girls. It took them three or four days in a hotel in Omaha before they could venture out to return to their home, which was a five-hour drive. However, as friends and family came and saw their little Paula, everyone realized that this was the perfect child to be a little sister to Megan and Sidney. Their family was complete.

Their last trip was not picturesque like the one in Beijing, and it was not as much fun, but generally everything went well, and they returned home with their newly made family of five. They definitely felt the hand of God in accumulating their family. The last arrangements in China were made by a committee of five people who acted godlessly and without much compassion in working the adoptions, placements, and assignments within the Chinese system. The provinces vary in the availability of Christians and churches, which affected how they were treated.

Larry mentioned how interesting it was that all parents they knew who had adopted from a foreign country had bonded first with the child's photo, which they had received from the adoption agency. What a change for that chosen baby! Before adoption, those babies were often born and abandoned with a note on their clothes. In the Lennox family, the immediate bonding over a photo started the love flowing from parents to child, and this love continues to grow.

Turning to You

"How great is the love the Father has lavished on us, that we should be called children of God! And that is what we are!" (1 John

3:1). God adopts us into His family when we knock on His door. How awesome is that! Now Larry and Melody have adopted three girls into their family. They can show the girls parental love because God has showed them how. "We love because he first loved us" (1 John 4:19). Jesus makes us all brothers and sisters. "You are all sons of God through faith in Christ Jesus, for all of you who were baptized into Christ have clothed yourselves with Christ. There is neither Jew nor Greek, slave nor free, male or female; for you are all one in Christ Jesus" (Galatians 3:26–28).

Prayer

With You, Lord, there is no difference between Chinese or American or any other nationality. Thank You for parents who adopt foreign children and raise them as their own. Amen.

Reason 4

Adoptions Offer Parents Choices

13

Open Adoption Shows Love and Trust

Sue and Dale Vagts

Can you imagine holding your little baby for a few hours or a few days and then being strong enough to say, "I can't raise this child right now. I am handing this child to you because I have come to know you, and you will be a good parent for my child."

Sue and Dale Vagts watched this scenario three times. It was never easy when they made an agreement with the birth parents. They promised to do everything possible to raise that child in the way they had discussed. This trust took a long time to develop when Sue and Dale adopted their first two children. They didn't have the benefit of plenty of time when they adopted their little Sarah to complete their family of three children.

The trust between adoptive and birth parents was more a covenant than an agreement. Dale felt that this was so because they were dealing with the life of a person, a soul. Jennifer Crissman Ishler, who developed a study curriculum about adoption, said, "You don't give up a baby like you give up smoking. You place a baby in a *home*."

The young couple graduated from college, got married, and settled in Lincoln, Nebraska. Of course, they planned to have children, but that didn't happen. After a while, they decided to find out if there was medical help available for them. First, Sue was tested for fertility, and then Dale. They found out that he had no sperm count, which was a result of maturation arrest, a somewhat uncommon problem in infertility. Questions arose. What did this mean for them? Would they be open to adoption? Would she want to be impregnated with someone else's sperm? Since they were a couple, was the use of someone else's sperm anti-marriage? Wouldn't they both want to have the same experience? Sue and Dale also had a very strong faith, and they considered what God would want them to do. They often prayed about this decision.

One night at Sue's Toastmasters club, someone gave a speech about the process of open adoption. She went home and told Dale about it, to which he said, "It sounds crazy. Why would a child have both adoptive and birth parents in its life?" They continued to consider the closed adoptions they had known about, but they slowly warmed up to the idea of their adopted child seeing and knowing his or her birth parents. They read, read, and read books and more books about adoptions, exploring all angles of adoption. Eventually they went to a highly recommended adoption agency.

This brought them to a group meeting in Omaha, Nebraska. They heard different panelists talk about being adopted in various situations. Birth parents and adoptive parents talked about their situations in both closed and open adoptions. This was very eye-opening for Dale and Sue. Maybe open adoption *was* for them. So they prepared a portfolio and started the process.

To their surprise, they were selected quickly. In February they started having sessions every Sunday with an expectant mom, who gave birth in April. The mother of the baby trusted them enough to ask them to be in the delivery room when Matthew Caleb was born. They were so excited about this possibility that they worked overtime and into the night hours to be ready when the baby was born. They even went to the expense of getting a pager for the express purpose of receiving the call to go immediately to the hospital. The Sunday night before Matt was born, they were both at the office. It didn't dawn on their social worker that they would be at the office at midnight, so she left five frantic messages at their home phone instead of paging them. Thankfully, Matthew hadn't been born yet, and they arrived in time for his birth at 7:30 a.m.

Immediately after Matthew was born, the birth mom held him lovingly for a few minutes. She then granted Sue the first chance to hold him and said, "Matthew, I want you to meet your mother." The strength that she showed in this selfless act was unbelievably beautiful. The birth father was difficult to get in touch with, and he hadn't yet signed relinquishment papers. The birth mom was sure she could not raise the child alone, but she loved the baby. However, she could not release him until the birth father had relinquished him. Even though Dale and Sue took Matthew home from the hospital, they only had foster parent credentials. They continued to keep in touch with the birth mom, and she continued to tell them that she supported the adoption.

Finally, after eight days, the birth father relinquished his parental rights. Dale, Sue, and Matthew drove to Omaha to spend the afternoon with the birth mom, and all the legal paperwork was finalized. Dale and Sue were dripping with emotional tears over the birth mother's strength in giving this beautiful baby boy to them to raise. The experience of being in the room while Matthew was born will forever be locked into their memories as one of the most significant times of their lives. This time was a gift of enormous proportions.

When Matthew's birth mom was discharged from the hospital, Sue and Dale were there with her. This was the moment when Dale and Sue would take Matthew home for good. The birth mom asked for the hospital band that was around the little boy's arm. At this point, Sue and Dale realized the unfairness of it all: they were taking the live baby, and the birth mother was taking the band. This physical exchange signified the covenant between parents that this was right for this baby at this time. They all knew that this child would be raised by Sue and Dale, but the birth mom and dad would have opportunities to have a relationship with this dear child. The mother would be able tell Matthew later that she hadn't wanted to give him up but that she had chosen his parents very carefully. They had chosen his name together, but Sue and Dale would be raising him.

This mom knew that she could proceed with her life, and that Matthew would be raised by loving parents where she could watch him grow into a fine young man—which he is now at age eighteen. What a blessing of open adoption!

Sue and Dale never tried to keep their children from their birth parents, but distance was sometimes a challenge. When Matthew was nine and in fourth grade, Sue had a conference in San Antonio where his birth mother lived. After calling ahead of time, they were able to arrange being in the same hotel, and they went to Sea World together. While Sue was in meetings, Matthew was able to spend time with his birth mother.

Matthew's birth mother knew that his father was also in San Antonio, and she notified him that he could visit Matthew. At first the response was no, but as time went on, she got a call from him saying that he would like to see Matthew. At this point, she told Matthew that he would get a chance to see his father also. This made Matthew very nervous, and when his father came, Matthew went into the bathroom. He finally came out and was able to spend the day with his biological mother and father. Because of the covenant-like relationship Sue and Dale had with Matthew's parents, they knew that Matthew would be back with them, safe, at the end of the San Antonio trip.

Sue had an awesome experience with Matthew. He was a very expressive child, and when he was two years old, she read many,

many books to him. At one point they saw a skyline of a city in a book. Matthew pointed out that this building represented his adoptive father, another his birth father and mother, another his adoptive mother, and so on through his family.

One game he liked to play was to cover himself with a blanket and have his mother sit above him. She would talk about having her new baby duck, saying how she would love and care for him. Then Matthew would jump out from under the blanket as if he was being hatched. Matthew loved this game and asked Sue to do it over and over again. Sue never minded, because she felt that it was Matthew's way of feeling like he had been born to her.

Sue and Dale knew that Matthew's birth mom wanted him to be in a family with brothers and sisters. After experiencing the joy of having a baby in the home, they were both ready to start the process again to find a sister or brother for Matthew.

This second relationship between the birth mom and dad and the expectant adopters grew with each meeting. Matthew, who was over one year old, was able to participate. The birth parents for their second child were not married, so Dale and Sue met with them separately.

One set of grandparents entered into the picture and were ready to be grandparents, adding a new development. They had two children but no grandchildren yet. Allowing this first grandchild to leave the family was not a happy thought in their minds. They had offered to raise the baby themselves. After they came to know Sue and Dale, the process continued toward adoption. Sue and Dale offered to work with the birth parents to find a name for the baby, which they had done before they'd adopted Matthew. It was a little harder with all four parents giving suggestions, but they ended up with Paul Zachary. Dale was happy to continue with biblical names.

This time the delivery was very different. The Vagts were called when labor started, but it was twenty-two hours before they got the next call asking them to come and see the new baby boy. The birth mom came from a large, close-knit family. The birth mother's mother had made her write to all her aunts and uncles to tell them that she was pregnant and was placing the baby up for adoption at birth. The birth mom stayed in the hospital with the baby the first night. The second night, she took him home and recorded his baby sounds and enjoyed being with him. She felt she needed time to say hello to the baby before she had to say good-bye.

They held a Mass at the grandparents' home, with some eighty people in attendance. It was kind of awkward because some of the people were not supportive of the adoption. However, after Paul spent the night with his birth mother, she brought him to Sue and Dale the next day and signed the adoption papers.

When they walked away with Paul, Sue and Dale could see how weak his mother was, to the point of needing help to walk, and yet she was so strong in knowing that she had done the right thing by him. On the second Thanksgiving after the adoption, Sue and Dale received a letter from her that said how happy she was that Paul was exactly where she wanted him to be.

Paul's birth father felt way outnumbered at these events and did not attend the Mass. On the same day, he had many family members gathered for a funeral, and he asked Sue and Dale to bring the baby to meet them. Can you imagine how uncomfortable this was for all involved? This man, however, took his position as the birth father very seriously, and he continues to spend some time with his child. Dale, Paul, and his birth father spent a day golfing not long ago. As usually happens when another person comes into the picture, the birth father's family stepped back when he got married to a lady who wasn't the birth mom.

Dale was diagnosed with testicular cancer about the time they wanted to adopt again, but after treatment, he received a clean bill of health. They didn't know if this would prevent them from further adoptions. They proceeded as before and soon found out that there was a sixteen-year-old girl who was pregnant. At about seven months into the pregnancy, the girl finally told her grandmother that she was going to have a baby. Her parents learned about the baby from the grandmother, and they felt that adoption was a good solution. They knew that their daughter was not ready to be a parent.

Sue and Dale's relationship with this family suffered, as they did not have as much time to get to know the birth parents. The biological father had only one week's notice of the adoption. Naming the baby with the birth parents was a little more difficult this time. Their relationship was not as amicable, and there were some disagreements. The birth father finally made some concessions and agreed to Sarah, even though he already had a sister and a step-niece named Sarah.

Meeting with the teenage birth parents, the two sets of parents who were still parenting the birth parents, and the set of grandparents—all separately—was quite a feat. As time went on, the older boys, Matthew and Paul, had almost a grandparent-grandchild relationship with Sarah's birth father's parents. The boys and their sister, Sarah—the actual biological granddaughter—are all welcome at Sarah's grandparents' home.

Sue and Dale had an opportunity to view family adoptions from the other side when his niece was considering placing her baby for adoption. She consulted Sue and Dale before she had the baby, and the adoption proceeded. They felt fortunate to experience the other side. Sue and Dale go camping with a couple who have two adopted children and one who is not adopted. At one point, they heard the biological child complain, "Where is my birth mom? I want one too."

Dale was disappointed when he found out that he could not have biological children, but several things happened to wipe that feeling from his thoughts. His beautiful wife, Sue, chose to adopt rather than to have sperm implanted in her, so that she could share an identical experience with her husband. What a treasure to have love like that in your home! While raising his children—who are now eighteen, sixteen, and twelve—he has come to enjoy seeing how they resemble their parents in actions and looks. "What a trite thing to have wanted my children's faces to look like mine," Dale now says.

Sue and Dale watch their children interact with their birth parents, and they are glad to see them have this loving relationship with the ones who gave them life. It strengthens them all to see humans work together in complete understanding of the reproductive system that God created, in order to provide solutions when the unexpected pregnancy happens. Sue and Dale realize the blessing that their birth families are and always will be. Their family is complete now, including all the connecting families.

Turning to You

God knew you before you were conceived and before you were born. If He knew about Jesus before He was conceived, He could also know about you. "On the eighth day, when it was time to circumcise him, he was named Jesus, the name the angel had given him before he had been conceived" (Luke 2:21). He made you in the womb. "This is what the LORD says—your Redeemer, who formed you in the womb: I am the LORD, who has made all things, who alone stretched out the heavens, who spread out the earth by myself" (Isaiah 44:24). What an amazing thing for God to reveal to us!

These are the words of a hymn written by Carolyn Winfrey Gillette to the tune of Nettleton 8.7.8.7 D ("Come, Thou Fount of Every Blessing").

> Long ago, when Pharaoh's daughter walked along the riverside,
> In a basket in the water was a baby, snug and dry.
> Tiny baby! Did his mother give him up so he might live?
> Love that gives to save another is a mighty love to give.
>
> Christ, you offered us a blessing—what our life in you can be:
> When a child is given welcome, then you also welcome me.
> In a world where children suffer and where all need love and care,
> Love that leads us to each other is an answer to our prayer.

Ready or Not

God, you call us your own children; we're adopted! We're reborn!
We rejoice that through adoption, human bonds are also formed.
Bless the ones who welcome children; bless the ones who let them go.
May each child be loved and welcomed; may each church help families grow.

—Hymn text: Copyright © 2014 by Carolyn Winfrey Gillette.
All rights reserved. Used by permission.
www.carolynshymns.com

Prayer

In the story of these adoptions, we see the strength of the birth parents as they released their children to be raised by Sue and Dale. We thank You for them. We thank You for Sue and Dale, who were willing to be open and allow the birth parents to visit their child. We see in the words of the hymn by Carolyn Winfrey Gillette that Moses' mother experienced the same sacrifice. These babies were all provided life in abundance because of the unselfishness of their parents. Thank You for these parents. Amen.

14

Love Is the Reward of a Life Decision

Gary and Erica White

Eric is fifteen years old now and doesn't live with his biological parents, Gary and Erica White. He was delivered on his mother's seventeenth birthday. His parents broke the mold that says that high school sweethearts usually don't end up getting married. They knew that they would not be able to take care of Eric, so they contacted the Nebraska Children's Home and attended monthly counseling. They realized that trying to parent—with their young emotions and their immaturity—wouldn't be fair to this wonderful child.

Gary and Erica White made their decision. Eric, their unborn baby, would be raised by another couple—who were married, wanted a baby, and were ready to be parents. So, the task of choosing Eric's parents began. Can you imagine the emotions running through these young parents' minds? In the meetings that followed, they met a couple they liked, and they started to form a personal attachment with them. The relationship between the two couples grew in understanding.

At the time of delivery, the adoptive parents asked to be in the delivery room, but at the time, this was impossible for the Gary and Erica. It was very difficult for them when the baby couldn't stay with them the night of the birth because of legalities. However, the foster parents caring for the baby allowed him to be with them the night before he was taken to his new home.

The young birth couple was hurting, confused, and full of love for the baby who was the product of their love for each other. This was a very difficult time for them. They had gone through the shame of an unwed pregnancy, initially without telling their parents. At the hospital, the grandma, who was ready to be a grandma, was in tears. She said she would help them in any way she could in their decision. Knowing that they would be able to visit the child right from the beginning was a bright spot in everyone's eyes. By this time, some of Gary and Erica's friends were at the hospital to give support, as they had been there for the young couple from the beginning.

Eventually Gary and Erica graduated and went to Las Vegas to be married. They had continued seeing Eric, their son, and when he was four years old, all the walls between the two couples fell. They trusted each other, and they no longer used the Nebraska Children's Home as a go-between.

Two sisters, now age twelve and four, were born to Gary and Erica. They always knew they had a big brother. The older girl looks very much like Eric, and both girls have a good brother-sister relationship with him. In fact, Eric now gets to choose when he goes to be with his White family. The Whites are respectful of the adoptive parents' feelings, and Eric loves them as parents. They had no other children but Eric. The adoptive mother was also adopted because her mother hadn't been able to have children.

The beauty of this story is that Eric always knew who his biological and his adoptive parents were. At one time, as a child, Eric said to Erica, "I was in your tummy." Today, Eric is six feet tall and continues vacationing every summer with Gary, Erica, and his sisters.

The Whites had friends who had a closed adoption and finally found their child, but legal restrictions on the closed adoption dictated that they could not see their child for two more years. Eric enjoys his siblings; his adoptive family has raised a wonderful son; and Gary and Erica have a son and brother for their girls.

What a wonderful ending to a difficultly timed pregnancy. Eric was given life. The biological parents were mature enough to show their love by using adoption. The adoptive parents were mature enough to allow the child to receive love from the biological parents. This maturity allowed Eric to have a larger family that included two sisters. Communication relieved fears that were obviously visible at times. "There is no fear in love. But perfect love drives out fear" (1 John 4:18a).

Turning to You

Jennifer Crissman Ishler, who developed a college class on adoption at Pennsylvania State University, said this: "Every child deserves a loving home, no child should be without a family and none should be abandoned." Gary and Erica believed these things, and they knew that they were not ready to get married. They overcame their fear, learned about open adoption, and gave Eric the greatest gift they could: a married mom and dad. This option is available to you.

Prayer

Thank You, Lord, for opening up adoption, which gave the Whites an opportunity to continue a relationship with their son after he was adopted. Also, thank You, God, for creating marriage so that children have a safe place to grow up. "'Haven't you read,' he replied, 'that at the beginning the Creator made them male and female and said, "For this reason a man will leave his father and mother and be united to his wife, and the two will become one flesh." So they are no longer two, but one. Therefore what God has joined together, let man not separate'" (Matthew 19:4–6). Amen.

15

Ready to Love a Child

Allison and Rich Lehr

After being married awhile, Allison and Rich decided to find out why they weren't having children. As teachers, they loved kids and were around them all the time. They met with doctors and tried several options that would help them have a baby. Nothing seemed to help. They decided that both of them were open to adoption. They learned about the Nebraska Children's Home in Omaha, Nebraska, which is the only agency nationwide that doesn't charge fees to the adopting parents. They have a large following of donors, which pays for their services.

Allison and Rich went through all the training required and put in their application to be adopting parents. At first, they were skeptical of open adoptions. As they learned more and more about how open adoption worked, they began to feel that open adoption was more beneficial to the child's needs. They were in tune with what was best for the child, and they decided they would accept open adoption terms.

It still took between one and two years before the letter they wrote to prospective birth parents was chosen and they were called.

They received some information about the birth mother and were able to meet Carol and the birth father, Jim, before their child was born. They were impressed by Carol's expressed thinking process of intelligence over emotion, or "I over E." Carol wanted to follow intelligence rather than emotions in deciding what to do for her unborn baby. Allison and Rich realized then how much Carol loved her baby, even before it was born. They also understood that Carol knew she was not in a position to raise her baby at that time. Even though Carol wanted I over E, Allison and Rich were not totally sure which letter would win in Carol's mind.

The call came on a day when their school had a track meet. The child was born, and Carol and Jim still wanted to place their little girl with Allison and Rich. They quickly went to the hospital before the track meet to see the baby that would become their daughter. What a day for them! They knew that in two days they would be going back to pick up a beautiful infant and bring her into their home. They named her Isabelle.

Allison says she cannot imagine the willpower it took for Carol and Jim to hand over their little girl to Allison and Rich. The time of choice was now at hand, but being able to follow the life of their child, in spite of the fact that they could not raise it, might have softened the reality of it all for Carol and Jim. They signed the papers, and Allison and Rich took Isabelle home.

Carol came to see Isabelle once or twice a year and at Christmas for a while, but the visits slowly dropped off as Carol went on with her life. Isabelle recently needed some genetic family history information. Since she is now twelve years old, Allison told her to call her birth mom and ask her. Carol easily answered the questions. The open adoption has prevented secrecy, and the questions Isabelle has from time to time have been quickly answered for her.

Allison and Rich wrote a letter to the Nebraska Children's Home stating that they would be willing to adopt again if some birth parent chose their file. Being a busy family, with both parents working and a two-year-old in the house, the thought of another adoption wasn't on their minds every day. Rich was at work when the next call came for them to consider taking a little boy who was four months old. Rich knew he had to reach Allison, who was on a field trip with her class. Finally he got through to Allison, but he couldn't talk. He was so happy about the possibility of getting another baby that he was crying. The excitement of having a son to be a sibling to their little girl was so great. He needed to talk with Allison, but it was hard to enunciate the words he needed to explain about the call. Finally Allison realized what Rich was trying to tell her, and they arranged to go and see the little boy the next day. They tried to think exactly what a four-month-old boy would look like and how that would be different from taking a newborn infant home.

Rachel, Eli's birth mother and a single mom, had two girls, ages four and two, who kept her busy. She did not think she could raise this baby too. She had made an adoption plan and had chosen another couple to raise him, but it had fallen through. This situation made Rachel think that she might be able to care for Eli. After two or three weeks, Rachel had come to believe that it was not possible for her to keep him and give him the care he needed. She had a sister in a nearby town who had friends who were excellent foster parents. Eli was placed with Stuart and Celia in a foster care situation. These foster parents had older children and soon realized that Eli needed a permanent home rather than temporary foster care. They came to love little Eli in the time they had him.

These foster parents took Rachel under their wing and said she should make a permanent decision about a home for Eli. Stuart and Celia did not feel prepared to raise him. Rachel had a hard time deciding, but she knew that Stuart and Celia were right. Eli needed a permanent, stable home. After learning about open adoption, Rachel decided that it would work for her, as she could still see Eli from time to time. The call was placed to Rich by the agency, and he called Allison. Eli was biracial but the discussion about whether race mattered to Rich and Allison had been answered long ago. Yes, they would adopt Eli. After adoption, they named the little boy Alex.

Allison and Rich now had a brother for Isabelle. This adoption was quite different, as Alex did not show a lot of emotion for most of his first year. Allison and Rich attribute this to the fact that he had been in three different homes before he was five months old. He needed time to adjust to this new family. Today he is a delightful child and is well adjusted because of the love and stability his adoptive parents have given him.

Alex's birth mother met with him and his adoptive family off and on for a while, and Allison, Rich, and Alex have been to Rachel's home. They met his two older half sisters and eventually met Rachel's new husband and two more half siblings. Alex's birth father has never been in the picture. When Alex has questions, Allison tries to track down Rachel, but most of the time, she is not able to find her. They have photos of Rachel and her family, and Alex is content with the answers Allison is able to give him. Allison and Rich's parents are grandparents who are very active in Isabelle and Alex's lives. This gives another dimension of love, which surrounds them on a regular basis.

These open adoptions relieved the birth parents' fears that they would never see their children again, and the arrangement has worked well for both sets of parents. The wishes of the parents have been honored, and brotherly love is evident in this family.

Turning to You

Stuart and Celia stay in touch with Alex, as they truly fell in love with him as foster parents. Rich and Allison have had the opportunity to be loving parents because of the gift given to them by Isabelle and Alex's birth parents. Carrying a baby, giving it life, and allowing it to be adopted are truly the best gifts that a parent who is not ready to be a parent can give. In this instance, the adoptive parents and the adopted child win. All these parents extended true love by choice. "Love must be sincere. Hate what is evil; cling to what is good. Be devoted to one another in brotherly love. Honor one another above yourselves" (Romans 12:9–10).

Prayer

Dear Lord, help us to love and cling to what is good, even in the most difficult of situations. Be with all these parents as they go forward, and bless Isabelle and Alex. Amen.

Reason 5

Agencies Choose Adoptive Parents Carefully

16

God Works for the Good of Those Who Love Him

Bill and Michelle Michener

Bill and Michelle, after a few years of marriage, decided to have children. Nothing happened for seven years. The fertility drugs didn't help. They decided to adopt after Bill heard about the Nebraska Children's Home Society at his Kiwanis meeting. They were attracted to this society because it is a nonprofit agency that pairs children who need homes with parents who want children. It is funded by donations, money from estates, and fundraisers.

In his work with troubled teens, Bill sees the results that occur when a parent doesn't know how to care for the child. He believes there is a need for all parents to take parenting classes. Because of this, he did not mind undergoing background checks in order to adopt children. He and Michelle had to be approved by the Federal Bureau of Investigation (FBI), Nebraska state investigators, and child abuse and neglect monitors.

The Micheners took an introductory class for adoptive parents at the Children's Home Society and found out that the competition was tough. More parents are looking for children than there are babies to go around. The society weeds out those who are not truly interested in raising children. The parents' answers to criteria are entered into a pool or bucket, and the birth mother reviews them. By the time the Micheners decided to adopt, they had already lost three of their own parents. They soon realized that their parents' wisdom would have helped them answer many questions. These are some of the items that required information from the Micheners about themselves and family members:

1. Explain your discipline ideals.
2. Explain your spiritual beliefs.
3. Is there alcohol use in your family?
4. Were you abused as children, or was abuse in your family?
5. Have you used drugs, or was drug use in your family?
6. Describe the health history of you and your parents.
7. What do you like to do with your free time?
8. Describe your family life.
9. Detail your education.
10. State hobbies that are practiced in your extended family.
11. How long have you been in your home?

Michelle had to practice patience because she knew that the sooner she got her answers turned in, the sooner they could be put into the pool of potential parents. She was motivated, and it took her one day to fill in her answers. Bill was challenged by the process and took a month to complete his. After they completed the work, they were assigned a caseworker, and the background checks started.

The questions became tougher, as they had to divulge much about themselves and their lives. They felt that everything about them was open to the world because of questions like these: What are the hardest things you deal with in your marriage, individually and together? Have you mourned not being able to have children? What age range are you willing to adopt?

Then they had counseling sessions, individually and as a couple. Bill's background is in counseling. He graduated from Doane College, and for five years he has been a professional, licensed mental health practitioner. This experience helped him, but Michelle felt that she had emptied her entire life and that there was nothing private left.

Bill and Michelle found this process of adoption to be very hard work. They saw promises made but never kept. They attended a six-week parenting class that covered diapering a baby to CPR (cardiopulmonary resuscitation). They were encouraged to attend classes where birth parents and adoptive parents talked with each other. This whole process started in July of 2005 and finished in early January of 2006. In January they opened their home for in-home studies, at which time the caseworker came to the house to interview them and check their home for babyproofing and safety. Bill and Michelle wanted to know when they should start preparing a room for their baby. It was depressing to hear that some couples had been in the pool for ten years before deciding not to adopt at all.

This did not deter them, and they chose Winnie the Pooh characters and a green theme to decorate a baby room. Everything was done in preparation for adoption, so they anxiously waited for their letter of approval. It was now February, eight months after they had started with the children's home. Bill called the caseworker every week to see if their information had been shown to birth mothers. Michelle knew that he was calling, and he helped her to calm down each time there was no news. Michelle is a wonderful, active person who is used to seeing things get done quickly, and she was stressed by the wait and by the excitement of possibly being a mother.

Michelle's mother wanted to give them a baby shower after they had been in the pool for a month and a half. Even though this didn't seem like the best idea when they didn't have a baby yet, there was no stopping her. This grandmother-to-be prepared a list of invitees and sent out invitations to their family and friends. Michelle wondered what other people would think about having a baby shower when they didn't even have a baby yet. The shower happened. Bill had been anxiously calling the caseworker through the months of February, March, April, May, and June. Thank goodness that Bill and Michelle had friends at Bill's work—Pete and Maureen Allman—to visit with them and help them be patient. The Allmans had already been through this process.

Finally, the caseworker called with good news: a birth mother wanted to meet them. She was at the Nebraska Correctional Center for Women in York, Nebraska. She was seven months pregnant and had found out about her pregnancy after being incarcerated. As quickly as they could, Bill and Michelle drove to the correctional center in York. They had to pass inspections before they could enter. In a private room in the center, they met the spirited young pregnant lady, and they got along immediately. She decided that day that Bill and Michelle could have her baby and would raise it in a manner she liked. The pregnant lady could not keep her baby at the center. She knew she must either place her baby for adoption or have her own parents take care of the child until she was released. Her parents were already raising a son born to this daughter. They could not care for another baby at their advanced age.

While they were meeting at the center, the birth mother and Bill and Michelle talked about numerous subjects concerning the baby. They decided to come up with boys' and girls' names together. Both parties wanted a name that they mutually agreed upon. When the session was over, Michelle was so wound up that they decided to go golfing to calm down. They went back a week later with four boys' names and four girls' names. The birth mother had forgotten her list, but she went back and got it. They waited. Peyton was on both lists for a boy. In their discussions, they decided on Michael as a middle name, as this name had been in both families. Later, the Michener's added Lee to his name also. The baby became Peyton Michael Lee Michener.

Now the waiting was almost impossible. In mid-July they received a call from the caseworker saying that the birth mom was leaking amniotic fluid. This meant that the birth might be early. No, they didn't need to come now. The center would keep Bill and Michelle posted. The birth mother wasn't due until August, but a week and a half later, the doctor scheduled an emergency C-section. Bill and Michelle were told to be at the hospital at 6:00 a.m. on that morning. They decided to drive to York and check into a hotel so they could be at the hospital on time.

Now some unbelievable things happened. Michelle lost her wedding ring. She was so wound up that she couldn't think clearly. They searched and searched for the ring. Not once in their excitement did they think about coming back to get it later. They didn't arrive at the hospital until 7:00 a.m. They thought that because of their late arrival they would have missed the whole birth. But this was not so, for the baby was born healthy at 7:29 a.m. with some amniotic fluid in his lungs. The birth mother had the doctor leave some of the umbilical cord so Bill could cut it. Bill and Michelle could hardly believe this beautiful child. They wanted to hold him right away. The birth mom looked at them and said, "Michelle, pick him up." Michelle's heart was warmed by this tender thought from the birth mother.

Bill and Michelle fell in love with Peyton instantly. Because of the incarceration, none of their families were able to be in the hospital. They had a hospital room and had Peyton with them. They changed his first diaper. They put him to sleep in bed. He woke up. Michelle was so tired, she wondered, "What have I gotten myself into?" They looked at the baby and again felt the love only a parent can feel. They gave him his first bath and had him circumcised. The birth mom wanted them to make that important decision.

The birth mother had an estranged relationship with her parents. However, her mom and sister came to meet Bill and Michelle. All were pleased that Peyton was going to great new parents who could care for him. Then they were presented with one more bridge to cross. The caseworker said that the birth father had contacted her and was curious to know about Peyton. As required by law, he had seventeen days to call and stop the adoption. If he didn't take action by that time, his nonaction was just as formal as signing the papers.

Finally, the family could meet Peyton. There was a welcoming party waiting for them. After this joyous time, they waited seventeen more days, travelled to York, and were very relieved when the birth mother signed the papers. Bill and Michelle took their baby, Peyton, home for good. It was hard to believe that this beautiful boy was now in their care and was their son. They worried about SIDS (Sudden Infant Death Syndrome) and followed the doctor's orders to have the baby sleep on his back. But Peyton wouldn't sleep on his back, so they took turns having him sleep on his stomach on top of them. They continued this practice, saying, "It's my turn," and changing places during the night for approximately eight months. Their dreams had come true, and they were going to do whatever it took to be sure this baby was safe.

Bill and Michelle sent pictures and letters about Peyton to the birth mother every week for about a year. Peyton's birth mother rarely responded. On March 27, 2007, the adoption was finalized. Peyton's last name was changed to theirs on the birth certificate, and they got the new birth certificate in the mail. Bill and Michelle Michener had received a wonderful gift from God: a healthy baby boy.

Turning to You

It is interesting that the baby wasn't born until Bill and Michelle arrived at the hospital. Romans 8:28 gives us an understanding that Bill and Michelle were called to be Peyton's parents. It says, "And we know that in all things God works for the good of those who love him, who have been called according to his purpose." We know that God is all-powerful and can arrange the time a baby is born.

In the Old Testament, Hannah prayed for a son. "God began making the necessary arrangements in response to what she had asked. Before the year was out, Hannah had conceived and given birth to a son" (1 Samuel 1:19–20a MSG). In Job 38:37–38, God said, "Who has the wisdom to count the clouds? Who can tip over the water jars of the heavens when the dust becomes hard and the clods of earth stick together?" Almighty God can, that's who. "Ah, Sovereign LORD, you have made the heavens and the earth by your great power and outstretched arm. Nothing is too hard for you" (Jeremiah 32:17).

Prayer

Thank You, Lord, for the regulations that make sure babies are placed in safe homes. Please help mothers who cannot raise their children at the time to understand that there are parents waiting for a baby to love, care for, and raise as their child. Release the fears of these women. Let them know that much joy may come in the future because of a reunion with their child as an adult.

Thank You, Lord, for Peyton Michener, who, to his adoptive parents' delight, often says that before he came, he was with God, waiting for them. Amen.

17

You Are My Real Mom, and I Love You

Linda Haun

Steve had been really sick as a young person, and he knew that having children might be difficult for him. Linda always knew that she wanted children, and she figured that in time Steve would too. It was a leap of faith that he would, and could, come to that realization.

A couple of years after Steve and Linda were married, they struggled with the constant demands of keeping her niece and nephew, ages five and two. They experienced the joy too. After keeping them, Steve realized that he wanted children, one way or another. He said there was something special about going into the children's bedroom and seeing them stretch their little arms out to him, wanting to be picked up out of their cribs. When he picked them up from day care, they would come running to him with open arms. Having little children trust them and give them so much love made a very good impression on both Steve and Linda.

Linda's sister in Iowa had a baby, which Linda adored. The possibility of adoption was in Linda's mind, as she had two adopted cousins and had watched them grow up as full family members. After a year or so, Steve too thought that having a baby would be pretty special. They went to fertility doctors, tried insemination, and had lots of tests. In the end, they found out that they both had fertility problems. They discussed the question of adoption and decided to go through Nebraska Children's Home. It took a year to attend all the meetings and decide if they wanted a closed or open adoption.

Their two adopted children are now twenty-three and twenty-six, and back then, open adoptions then were not like they are now. Then, the birth mom picked a family from forms filled out on their applications. The adopting parents' beliefs, financial stability, desire for children, and marital status were evaluated by the birth mother.

After two years of working with the children's home, Linda and Steve were starting to be concerned about their chances of getting a baby. Other couples were getting babies, and their friends were having babies. Linda saw mothers with several children who had no shoes. Linda could afford shoes for a child, but she couldn't have a child. Then one day Linda got a phone call at work. She was told that a three-week-old baby boy was available and had just become adoptable. They had less than twenty-four hours' notice.

Trent, their first adopted child, had wonderful grandparents, who knew that his birth mother, Lisa, was pregnant. They knew that she was struggling over what to do about the child. Lisa's mother had died, and her father and stepmother wanted her to place the baby for adoption. Lisa could not make up her mind. She wanted the best for the baby, but she wanted to be there for him herself. She took Trent to live with her aunt, who helped her. After Lisa realized that she wouldn't be able to care for Trent as a single mom, the baby was placed in foster care. Soon after that, Lisa signed the papers that would allow him to be adopted.

Linda and Steve fell in love with Trent at first sight. His brown eyes and brown hair resembled Steve, and some people say they look alike, but Linda says she doesn't see it. Kelsey, their second adopted child, looks more like Steve. But it didn't take long for these new parents to realize that who the baby looked like was insignificant. They totally accepted Trent and Kelsey as their own children. Kelsey's birth mom picked Linda and Steve because she wanted her child to have a stable family and not be an only child. She never told her parents that she was pregnant.

How did Steve and Linda get Kelsey? It wasn't easy. The children's home put childless couples ahead of those who already had a child. Steve and Linda knew their chances of getting another baby would be slim. Thank goodness that Kelsey's mom wanted her to be placed into a family.

Steve and Linda met the condition of an open adoption by going to the Children's Home when their children were one month old to meet the birth parent. They were able to meet Trent's aunt and mother and Kelsey's mom and grandparents. At that meeting they decided how open they wanted the adoption to be. They decided that all communication would go through the home and that they would share photos from time to time.

Letters came from Kelsey's birth mom for a while, which Steve and Linda shared with the kids. They read the Sesame Street book about Gordon and Susan's adoption to the children, which helped them understand the adoption process. Consequently, both Kelsey and Trent always knew that they were adopted. Steve and Linda were available to help them search for their biological parents when they turned eighteen. Kelsey said she might someday search for them, but Trent thought he would look for his real parents at age eighteen. So far, neither child has felt the need to know any parents other than Linda and Steve. If they become interested in knowing if they have step siblings, the open adoption would allow the Children's Home to let them have that information.

Infertility plays with a person's mind and self-assuredness. It tops any other statement to hear their adopted child say, "You are like my birth mom. You are my real mom. I love you. A birth mom is just biological." Neither birth mom sent photos, letters, or pictures after five years.

Steve and Linda's attachment to their adopted children proved very strong through the years. Today, Trent is a proud daddy himself. Linda tells Trent that she holds his baby through nap time. It is special "Linda time." She didn't even do that with Trent, though she waited so long to receive him. There is something special about holding a grandbaby. She can't even describe it. How fortunate Scott and Linda were to receive two healthy babies and to be able to be grandparents to their children's children.

Turning to You

Perhaps you understand the feeling of holding a grandchild. When God created us, He knew the feeling. "Children's children are a crown to the aged, and parents are the pride of their children" (Proverbs 17:6). "A good man leaves an inheritance for his children's children" (Proverbs 13:22). To leave someone what you have worked hard for tells of one's love for that person. A good man leaves more than money or belongings; he leaves character, teachings, and wisdom. Linda knows the joy of being a grandparent because two moms gave birth to children they couldn't raise. The birth parents gave the children life, and Linda was able to love them. And now she can hold a grandchild. Julie Henslee, a volunteer in a crisis pregnancy clinic, says, "There is no greater love on earth than to give your baby up for adoption."

Prayer

Lord, may You guide those who are not ready to be parents into giving life to the child and being brave enough to offer that child to a married couple that is ready to raise the child in a family. Thank

You, Lord, for showing us how special children are to You. "People were also bringing babies to Jesus to have him touch them. When the disciples saw this, they rebuked them. But Jesus called the children to him and said, 'Let the little children come to me, and do not hinder them, for the kingdom of God belongs to such as these. I tell you the truth, anyone who will not receive the kingdom of God like a little child will never enter it'" (Luke 18:15–17). Amen.

Reason 6

Children Love Parents Who Adopt Them

18

My Family History Is Love

Jim Budka

"If I'd had my choice of parents when I was adopted, I would have chosen these two as my parents," says Jim. This shows great love.

When the doctor said to Jim, "Tell me your family history," he shrugged his shoulders and said, "Your guess is as good as mine." Every time Jim asked where he had come from, he was told, "You were hatched on a fence post twenty miles south of Kansas City."

Today, Jim knows better than that. He knows that his original name was Clarence Ray Zichun, but the hospital mentioned on his birth certificate doesn't exist; the name doesn't appear in Kansas City phone books; there is no one by that name in the history books in his namesake town in Germany; and the name doesn't exist on Ancestry.com.

Jim's birth certificate shows his birthday as July 16, 1937, but he believes that might have been the day he was picked up by his adoptive parents. They renamed him James Robert Budka. James was the name of his adoptive father and grandfather, and the Czech language was spoken in their home. It was always nice to carry their name, as Jim was fortunate to have parents who really loved him. They did all that was possible for him, as far as their finances would let them.

There were multiple children in Jim's family. He had a stepsister, who was actually his cousin. His adoptive mother's sister had a daughter (Lois Holik) who came to live with the family after the sister died of cancer. This changed Jim's life because he had to move out of his bedroom and into the dining room. Lois had only been with them for a year when her father came to say good-bye to her. It seemed like a strange visit, but it made a little more sense to them when they heard that he had shot his girlfriend and then himself shortly afterward.

One day when Jim was seven years old, a friend came up to him at school and told him he was adopted. Jim called him a liar and asked where he got that crazy idea. His friend had learned it from another schoolmate, who had learned it from his mother, who had learned it from a friend of Jim's adoptive mother. Confronting his parents when he got home didn't make the orphan feeling go away. He was in tears, knowing that he was illegitimate.

Back then in the middle of the United States, no one ever talked about children being unwanted, and it was rare to be adopted. Jim's parents had to tell him the truth. First, they wanted to know how he had found out. They questioned him when he couldn't have been feeling worse. They thought they had been protecting him from a sad truth, but the protection was now removed. Jim thought that orphans weren't accepted. He felt like a throwaway from the orphan train that people had talked about. He hadn't been wanted by his own parents. As obstinate as he could be at seven years old, he blamed his adoptive parents, the very ones who had taken him in as their own, named him as one of the family, and formed their family around him.

The truth was that Jim's adoptive mother had had seven miscarriages and desperately wanted to start a family. His adoptive father responded by turning to liquor. The situation was exacerbated by the adoptive father's mother needing constant care, which took Jim's mother to an almost total collapse. At that point, a pastor, formerly a Presbyterian missionary, helped the family. As he was helping another friend adopt, he was able to place Jim with Mr. and Mrs. Budka. The pastor and Jim's adoptive parents bonded, and Jim had a lifelong friend in the making.

Had Jim not been told at school that he was adopted, he might soon have figured it out on his own. By age ten, he was taller than both parents. At that point, it didn't make any difference to Jim. He had accepted their love. He could now say, "If I'd had my choice of parents when I was adopted, I would have chosen these two as my parents."

As he has grown older and become wise in the world, Jim understands the pressure on a young woman without solutions to an unwanted pregnancy. She is very vulnerable, and he is saddened that his biological mother had to be in that position. He wishes that she could know that his adoptive parents took responsibility for him, provided a home, and taught him by their example how to live justly in this world. He was given every chance at a good life.

Today, Jim works many, many hours in his Presbyterian church in order to give back. This is because he is thankful that his parents made him who he is, which is plain ol' Jim. The congregation in his church is blessed every day because of the wonderful photos he takes of all the church events. There may not be a committee (Presbyterians have lots of committees) or position that Jim hasn't taken to do his part.

Turning to You

No matter what problems or structure your family has, think of all the good it provides you, and be thankful. Colossians 2:6–7 says, "So then, just as you received Christ Jesus as Lord, continue to live in him, rooted and built up in him, strengthened in faith as you were taught, and overflowing with thankfulness." You can trust the Lord for your needs. "The LORD will guide you always; he will satisfy your needs" (Isaiah 58:11).

Prayer

Dear Father in heaven, help us to be thankful for the family we have and not to envy others. Thank You for people like Jim, "hatched on a fence post," who found that the LORD provided all he needed as a baby and now shows us all how to trust in You today. Amen.

19

Discipline Is a Gift of Love

Gregory Pieper

There were five children in Art's family, and he was the second oldest. He and his brother Jessie took the brunt of their father's angry, drunken episodes. Both parents drank heavily, and Sylvia, their mom, was always verbally and emotionally abusive. The children were sent to school, but they received little help with homework and no encouragement to get involved in sports or other school activities. Things only got worse after their father passed away because of an alcohol-related illness. Sylvia continued to drink heavily and barely had time to care for the younger three children. Art and Jessie were never expected to be home at a certain time. In fact, they could not count on their mother being home on any particular night either.

Jessie decided that there was nothing for him at his home, and he joined the navy. Art was only sixteen when Child Protective Services came and took the kids away from their parents. Art then decided to lie about his age and was able to get into the army two years earlier than the required age of eighteen. Both Jessie and Art followed their parents' paths, taking up drinking at an early age and having children without giving them proper care and love. Jessie stepped in front of a car after a night at the bar and was killed. Art divorced his first wife and then was separated from his son Gregory and became homeless. He was fortunate that there was a lady who took in homeless veterans for only a small stipend. Art was able to earn this small amount of money, and he stayed with the lady for about six months—until his body gave out, and he died of a heart attack.

Now, perhaps you are wondering what happened to the three younger siblings of Art and Jessie. When Sylvia died, these three children were thirteen, ten, and eight years of age. There was a lady named Zola, who heard about the orphaned children. Zola loved children. She had adopted two children already, but she proceeded to go through the courts and adopt Lizzy, Alfred, and Tammy. It was a blessing that they were able to stay together.

At first, the children weren't sure that living as Zola's adopted children was a good thing. All of a sudden, someone was checking on their homework and making them get up early enough to get to school on time—and every day too. They had to help with shoveling the snow, mowing the lawn, and cleaning up the table after dinner. Zola demanded that their rooms be cleaned every Saturday. And they had to let Zola know where they were at all times, and they all had to be home for dinner at night.

These kids were bright. They complained some, but they soon realized that Zola cared about them and what happened to them. She encouraged them to be cheerleaders, to compete in spelling bees, to act in the school play, and to try out for sports. She came to watch them when they were in plays or played in a school sport. This wasn't easy for her, as one of her adopted children was a special needs child, and she was raising all five as a single mother. She took seriously the responsibility of being a parent, and the children began to love her for it.

After the firm love Zola gave to these three children, none of them followed the family's drunken past. Lizzy worked for the government and learned to love children too. She fostered a little boy and eventually adopted him. Alfred is raising his own family and owns a family business. Tammy has consistency and a good life working a steady job. They have continually provided for others and have been outstanding citizens in their community.

Gregory, being Art's son, witnessed how discipline made a difference in the lives of Lizzy, Tammy, and Alfred. He saw how alcoholism separated families and made adults distant from their children. Alcoholism also caused abuse and neglect within the family. When Gregory was little, his father often disappeared from the house. Sometimes he was gone for days. This became such a pattern that it caused his parents' divorce.

Zola came to Art's funeral. She came over to Gregory in tears, which he didn't understand. She had done so much for his aunts and uncle. Soon he realized what was upsetting her so much. She was sad that she hadn't been able to take Art, his father, into her home also. She realized that Gregory's life might have been different had Art experienced a more disciplined and loving style of life as a youth.

Gregory was always watching and learning how his family members disciplined their children. On his mother's side, he learned that his grandfather was adopted and had remained an only child. He had been spoiled and had grown up with little discipline. After marrying a woman he met in Japan and having two children, one of them Gregory's mother, he left and didn't participate in their upbringing. He was never able to put his kids first in his life. He left whenever a lady or an out-of-town opportunity came before him. Gregory's mother never saw much of her father or mother as she was growing up. Consequently, Gregory's mother had basically been raised by her grandmother, as was her brother, who was slightly mentally challenged.

The hurt experienced by Gregory's mother because of her absent father caused her to always refer to him as Gregory's grandfather instead of her father. Gregory learned from Zola the difference that love and discipline make. Because of her, he works in an organization that gives kids guidance. He understands that discipline makes a difference in young lives. The cycle has been broken.

Turning to You

Gregory saw these words of Jesus: "Come my children and listen to me" (Psalm 34:11). He listened to wise guidance and chose not to follow in the footsteps of his parents and grandparents. He realized that the human child, the only creature created in the image of God, needs love, care, protection, and discipline at a higher level than the birds of the sky do. "The wings of the ostrich flap joyfully, but they cannot compare with the pinions and feathers of the stork. She lays her eggs on the ground and lets them warm in the sand unmindful that a foot may crush them, that some wild animal may trample them. She treats her young harshly, as if they were not hers; she cares not that her labor was in vain, for God did not endow her with wisdom or give her a share of good sense" (Job 39:13–17).

Gregory was able to break the cycle of alcoholism, abuse, and neglect. "Do you not know that the wicked will not inherit the kingdom of God? Do not be deceived: Neither the sexually immoral nor idolaters nor adulterers nor male prostitutes nor homosexual offenders nor thieves nor the greedy nor drunkards nor slanderers nor swindlers will inherit the kingdom of God. And that is what some of you were. But you were washed, you were sanctified, you were justified in the name of the Lord Jesus Christ and by the spirit of our God" (1 Corinthians 6:9–11).

Prayer

Thank You for all the parents who choose to adopt children and give them love and discipline. Thank You for Your words in "the proverbs of Solomon son of David, king of Israel: for attaining wisdom and *discipline*; for understanding words of insight; for acquiring a *disciplined* and prudent life, doing what is right and just and fair; for giving prudence to the simple, knowledge and discretion to the young—let the wise listen and add to their learning, and let the discerning get guidance—for understanding proverbs and parables, the sayings and riddles of the wise" (Proverbs 1:1–6, emphasis added). Amen.

20

Love Kept Her from Anger and Blame

Cecelia Fredstrom

Cecelia knew from the beginning that she was adopted. Her brothers were adopted too. There was nothing strange about it. If the kids asked about their adoption, their parents told them everything they could. There wasn't much information, however, as the adoptions were secret. Cecelia remembers her mom always saying, "We didn't have to take you. We chose you." This made Cecelia feel that she was wanted and loved. She was always told that her birth mother loved her enough to provide a home for her with a mom and a dad. She understood that she had not been rejected. Since Cecelia had been an infant at the time, her mom couldn't have known her as a child or a grown-up, and no one knows the character of a small baby.

Cecelia was born on March 4 and was adopted in May at the age of two and a half months. It took some time because Cecelia's birth mother wanted her adoptive parents to be from South Dakota. She knew South Dakota people, and she felt that they would raise her child with a good sense of morality. The home for unwed mothers where Cecelia's pregnant birth mother had been sent was located in Denver, Colorado. Cecelia was an infant when she traveled with nurses to the Black Hills and on to Sioux Falls, South Dakota, where she was adopted.

Sometime after turning thirty and having three children of her own, Cecelia read the book *Waiting to Forget* by Margaret Moorman. Margaret had placed her child for adoption in the 1960s, at about the same time that Cecelia had been born. This mother had been about seventeen and had been forced by her family to release her child for adoption. After reading this book, Cecelia became more and more interested in books written from the standpoint of the birth mother. She knew she had to find her parents. The search was on.

Cecelia went directly to the Lutheran Social Services Agency, and for a fee of one hundred dollars, she could go in and look at the microfilmed papers of her adoption. Of course, the first stop was the courthouse, as she needed a judge to approve of this action. At the courthouse, she saw the name given to her by her birth mother and the legal documents between the participating parents. She saw her name as Heidi Ann Elfstrom. Her birth father was Norwegian. This was very exciting.

Her excitement would have ended at the courthouse except for the fact that the Lutheran Social Services documentation she had received showed that her birth mother lived in a small town in South Dakota. Another document showed that her birth mother was a freshman in college and was studying to be a teacher. A little more information indicated that the birth mother's father was a coach of a small college football team. This person would be Cecelia's grandfather.

Cecelia and her husband called the school and asked about the former football coach from the 1960s. The lady on the phone had been there a long time and soon told them that she knew his daughters. One of them had to be Cecelia's mother. The research was working!

Continuing to research, Cecelia called a friend in her mother's small town. When Cecelia told her friend her birth mother's name, the friend said she knew her. Cecelia moved fairly quickly, without writing a letter to her mother first. She called her on the telephone.

This call, completely out of the normal context of her mother's calls, really shocked her mother. Cecelia's birth mother remembered the exact words that everyone had said to her at age nineteen: "You can put this behind you. You can move forward and not have to worry." She had done what they'd said. How could this daughter have found her when all records were closed in the state documents? She needed answers before she could appreciate her daughter's research.

Not only had Cecelia's birth mother put this all behind her, but her husband knew Cecelia's birth father and did not like the man. Because of this, Cecelia has not met this man who is her stepfather. This negativity might have led to his wife's burying her thoughts about Cecelia. However, this birth mother responded to Cecelia's request and sent a manila envelope containing photos of her birth mother's life and family. Cecelia treasured those photos and still has them in the original manila envelope.

Cecelia also sent photos so that her birth mother could understand a little about who Cecelia is today. Cecelia is an extremely talented, well-adjusted person who has recently been hired into a very responsible position. It is easy for her birth mother to see the happiness, confidence, and beauty in the person she gave birth to so long ago. They continue to talk occasionally by phone and respond to each other by letters.

Cecelia actually got to meet her birth mother in 1997 in Sioux Falls, South Dakota. Cecelia likes her, but she doesn't crave more time with her. Let's just say that she did not find her mother to be a soul mate, like some other mother-daughter connections turn out to be. But Cecelia knows her biological roots and cares for her mother. Cecelia is delighted to have found her mother, and she believes that her mother is glad to have a daughter, as she only had boys in her marriage. Cecelia has her own close family, the one that raised her.

The birth mother knows now that she did not have to worry. Her daughter was raised by a wonderful mother and father. This birth mother has seen her beautiful daughter, heard about her happy childhood, and seen pictures of her daughter's children.

Cecelia downplayed all the research and information she found out about her birth parents because she didn't want her adoptive parents to feel jealous or slighted. They were wonderful parents to her. In fact, finding out about her birth parents has led her to be glad that she was raised in the family that adopted her. Cecelia didn't need to worry much, because the parents who raised her understood her curiosity.

Cecelia's adoptive mother had demonstrated many times that she did not want to think about her three adopted children's birth parents or their past names and history. When the adoptive parents were in the process of adopting Cecelia's brother, they were shown a paper that bore the baby's original name, and Cecelia's mother purposely neglected to remember it. The baby's original name, given to him by birth parents, was supposed to be blocked out. Cecelia's father clearly remembers seeing the name, but her mother had no recollection of seeing her son's other name.

Cecelia realized that she hadn't found out who her birth father was. When she located him, she wrote a letter instead of calling. He was thrilled and called her right away. This birth father wanted to meet Cecelia so much that he paid for her to fly to Portland, Oregon, to meet him. Her birth father introduced her to his wife, sons, and daughter. The daughter communicates with Cecelia and is the closest thing to a sister she has. Her birth father called to tell Cecelia when his wife died. This shows a great tenderness toward Cecelia.

When Cecelia flew to Portland, she realized on the way that although she had a biological connection with her birth father, she was essentially going to meet strangers. The birth father's wife was there and made conversation smooth, which made Cecelia comfortable. She looked at her father and realized that she resembled him as well as her birth mother. Any questions she had when she started her search were answered. This was good.

Cecelia didn't ask about the time when her birth parents realized that a baby was on its way. But her birth father had obviously thought about it over time. He told Cecelia that things might have been different if he hadn't been so dumb as a college freshman. He had known that he was going to see his girlfriend's father and that they had to tell him about the baby. He made the mistake of drinking too much and probably made a very bad impression. This ended any conversation about the couple getting married. Before that, he had definitely wanted to marry her.

Cecelia's birth parents are not active grandparents for Cecelia's children. Her birth mother met her children at ages four, three, and two. Her birth mother's three sons were in their twenties when they found out they had a half sister. Cecelia has never met the middle son. She has the closest relationship with the oldest son and exchanges Christmas cards with the youngest. Because of the birth mother's submission to her husband's wishes, no one in their small town knows about Cecelia. Cecelia understands that this is best and honors the situation, but she believes that her birth mother's sister has knowledge of the pregnancy.

Cecelia's curiosity has been appeased. She realizes that she has traits and actions that come from her adoptive parents as well as her birth parents. She believes that this knowledge, when shared, is heartening news for her adoptive parents. She is equally thankful to each set of parents, who gave her life and raised her well. The love she received kept her from wishing to change her circumstances, blaming anyone, or having any anger toward anyone.

Turning to You

This is an example of birth parents being found and curiosity being abated. The adoptive family obviously remains the main family for Cecelia. Cecelia was given life and has lived it to the fullest.

These are words of wisdom from an unknown first grader: "It [adoption] means that you grew in your mommy's heart instead of her tummy!" Joan Westphal, a grandmother of adopted children, says, "There is a lot to attribute to nurture and to nature in each child." When love is shown and individual people are respected at the time adopted children and birth parents meet, their lives change only as desired by all.

Prayer

Thank You, Lord, for the love children feel for their adoptive parents and family. You have made this possible because of Your wonderful creation of man and Your continued love and communication with us. "Show me your ways, O LORD, teach me your paths. Guide me in your truth and teach me, for you are God my Savior, and my hope is in you all day long" (Psalm 25:4). Amen.

21

One Born to Large Family Finds Love in Small One

Tom Tonack

The house was brimming with eleven children. An incident happened that killed one of the children, and the state welfare organization saw more trouble coming. The children were removed from the parents' home and were sent to live in a children's home. Eventually the brothers and sisters were split up, as some were adopted. A few of the older children were never adopted. Tom and his twin brother, Ted, were adopted about a year later and stayed together. They were not told where the other eight siblings lived, or whether those brothers and sisters were adopted or were raised in foster homes or the children's home.

An accident claimed the life of Ted, which had a dramatic effect on his twin, Tom. At that time, the twins' adoptive mother asked Tom if he would like to pursue looking for his siblings, which might soften the blow of losing his brother. Tom was not interested.

About the time that Tom was thinking of adopting his own child, a person called him, asking for Ted Tonack. Tom explained to the caller that Ted was deceased but that Tom Tonack lived there. That seemed to be enough information for the caller. Later, Tom received a letter from one of his sisters, who lived in the state of Nebraska where Tom lived. At this news, Tom's adoptive mother was a little worried that she might lose Tom too.

What actually happened was that Tom spent six months communicating with all eight of his siblings, getting to know them, and even having a family reunion with them. He spent hours in communication and then put the information on a shelf in his mind. Many of the siblings had led lives of struggle, shifting between foster homes, and having other difficulties. He found out the details of their lives—the tough tragedies, the divorces and illnesses, and the good things too. His biological mother and father had ended their marriage in divorce. After deciphering it all, Tom realized that he was the lucky one who had found love in his small adoptive family.

Turning to You

There are times when a child's adoptive home provides such a stable and loving atmosphere that the child's life is spared various struggles and tragedies. Tom learned that his adoption had provided an opportunity for him to have a successful life. His experience was a great background that led him and his wife to adopt a child themselves. Tom and Deloris treated both of their children as if they were made according to these verses: "So God created man in his own image, in the image of God he created him; male and female he created them. God blessed them and said to them, 'Be fruitful and increase in number; fill the earth and subdue it. Rule over the fish of the sea and the birds of the air and over every living creature that moves on the ground'" (Genesis 1:27–28).

Prayer

We praise You, Lord, for the couples who bring children into their homes and raise them as their own, giving them family and stability. Amen.

22

I Am Loved, and Life Is Full

Alice Lau

Alice's biological mother had more than she could handle. She was juggling a two-year-old daughter, school, and work. Becoming pregnant again was not in her plan. She thought about placing this new baby with a couple that was looking to adopt a child, but seeing the beautiful baby girl, she just couldn't let her go. She brought her home for a while.

This young mother soon realized that she wasn't able to provide what her baby needed. Alice's birth mother wanted her daughter in a permanent family where she would be cared for and loved. She chose to have Alice adopted in a closed adoption plan. The Nebraska Children's Home in Omaha arranged for a couple to adopt Alice. Just to make sure that Alice's mother was comfortable with her decision, they placed Alice in a foster home for a short while.

Alice believes that allowing her to be adopted by such great parents was the best gift her biological mother could have given her. She was so comfortable knowing that she was adopted and growing up with her parents that she didn't respond quickly to the request for contact by her biological mother when she was twenty years old. It took Alice a few months to decide what to do. She loved the parents who had raised her, so much so that she was concerned about how they would feel about her meeting her biological mother. This biological mother had never taken her to school, helped her with homework, or given her birthday parties as she grew up.

Alice's mother helped her write a letter to the biological mother, which included photos. This letter explained that she was happy and that she appreciated what had been done for her as a baby. Because of the gift of adoption, she had been able to participate in everything in school and church, and in other activities. She recognized the value of the gifts of life and adoption that she had received from her biological mother.

Alice's biological father never knew about her birth. Her biological mother responded to Alice's letter through the adoption agency and told her that her father was a piano player. This information helped Alice understand that he was one of the reasons she loved the music that her mother introduced to her.

Alice's biological mother sent news that another half sister had been born in a marriage that had ended in divorce. Because of this information, Alice connected the dots to realize that she had met the younger half sister at the Nebraska Wesleyan University Honor Choir while she was in high school. The university hosted a week-long choir made up of select students from around the state.

This has been the only correspondence Alice has had concerning these two half sisters because her own family makes her life full and happy. It was interesting information for Alice, who was raised as an only child, to find out that she was actually a middle child. Naturally, she wondered what it would have been like to have been raised in a family of three girls.

Alice is now married and is the mother of a young daughter named Sofia, who participates in the church music where Alice did as a child. Sofia's grandparents enjoy this little one and are blessed by her life as they were by Alice's life. This daughter even looks like her dad's mom. Alice realizes that she doesn't have her biological medical information, which might be useful someday to her daughter, but she knows she can get it if necessary.

Let's look at the gift given to Alice. She enjoyed the benefit of traveling to many places in the United States when her parents went on business trips. She was involved in sports, and she always had two parents at every event to love her through wins and losses. She experienced a stable home with parents who openly loved each other. These parents led her into a loving marriage and helped her interact with Sofia, her daughter. Alice believes that Sofia expressed affection early in her life because she saw love taught and lived.

Alice knows that she received love from her biological mother too. She loved Alice enough to let a childless couple adopt her, knowing that they could provide what the child needed. Her love enabled her to make that difficult choice. Alice states that she is glad her adoption was closed because she was spared the confusion of interacting with several parents. When she heard from her mother at age twenty, she was initially very upset that her biological mother had waited so long. Now, however, she realizes that it was good because she was old enough to make an informed decision about what kind of relationship she wanted to have with her biological family. Routine and consistency were part of the gift given to her, and she can pass that on to Sofia. This is easier to do because Alice provides one set of loving, adoring grandparents for her daughter.

The birth of her own daughter helped Alice see the love that her biological mother gave her. The acts of holding Sofia, caring for her, and loving her as mothers do has starkly revealed this truth to Alice. Alice believes that her parents taught her to be happy, and they are glad to know she has all the family she needs.

Turning to You

This story is a lesson in being happy in your circumstances, being thankful for gifts that have been given you, and proceeding to give love and provide blessings to those who have loved you and need your love now. Alice has the joy level described in John 15:9–12 because she is trying to obey the Lord's commands as her parents taught her. This verse says, "As the Father has loved me, so have I loved you. Now remain in my love. If you obey my commands, you will remain in my love, just as I have obeyed my Father's commands and remain in his love. I have told you this so that my joy may be in you and that your joy may be complete. My command is this: Love each other as I have loved you."

Prayer

Dear Father in heaven, please open our eyes to see the joy Alice has found. Bless us all as we strive to have faith as strong as Alice's. In Jesus' name, amen.

Reason 7

Parents Who Adopt Show Tremendous Love to Children

23

Mission of Love Began on Mission Trip

Tonya LaTorre

Tonya and her husband had four children, and their youngest was nine years old. You would think they would be looking forward to the empty nest days. However, she went on a mission trip to Uganda. Tonya spent her time there teaching about abortion.

She mentioned to friends that she might be interested in adopting a child from Uganda after she came home. Of course they told her, "Everyone wants to adopt after they work with the cute little ones. You will get over it soon."

Immediately after returning, Tonya told her husband about her thoughts of adoption. It seemed as if God wouldn't leave her alone. Her husband's answer made her realize that she wasn't the only one thinking about adoption. He said, "Sure, let's adopt two!" He then had to wait two more years for her to be ready to adopt.

It was amazing. Within two weeks, they had everything filed. It took only thirteen months total, not including spending six weeks in

Uganda to finish the adoption. They had a beautiful little girl, Kira, as part of their family for Christmas in 2011.

Tonya had fallen in love with the country of Uganda. She was devastated at the thought of all the other orphaned children because of the AIDS (acquired immune deficiency syndrome) epidemic in the country. They traveled to some of the other orphanages and found many children who did not have the excellent care that Kira had experienced before they adopted her. Now, when you are Tonya LaTorre, you don't let things slip by. She became impassioned about improving upon the typical Ugandan orphanage.

She and her husband set up a foster home in Uganda and turned it into a family home for sixteen children. Now, this didn't happen easily. They'd had money stolen by people who were working with them—as much as forty thousand dollars. The process turned out to be like a boot camp ritual of learning. They raised more money and proceeded carefully, eventually hiring college-educated individuals to run the home. Tonya visits the home four times a year and considers these sixteen children her own.

In the process of providing for these children, Tonya has hired a full-time mom, a person for medical care, a tutor, a cook, and a social worker with a degree in communication. Robert, the tutor, and Julie, the full-time mom, live in the home with the children. The home is called Kirabo Seeds. Kira gets to travel and see the children, whom she knows as her brothers and sisters. All the children in Kirabo Seeds know the English language, and they know about God's love. They are not available for adoption, because they have a home. Recently these children have reached out to the community, spreading the gospel in a variety of ways.

Just how do they have enough funding to supply everything these sixteen growing young Ugandans need? First, the home has five acres of land on which to grow their own food. All the children help in this process. Remember how you soaked up knowledge about what was going on around you when you were small?

Between Tonya's visits to Uganda, she raises funds in America. Everything she does is for the children. Funds are watched very closely, and when she tells a contributor that their three hundred dollars will be used for a particular child, she sees to it every one of those dollars is spent on that child. She and her older son, Jack, are in the process of traveling there at this time to check on everything and to provide love from our great country, the United States of America.

Tonya's generosity may not end with this venture. There is hope and a future plan to provide a village of homes for even more children. Kira, who is growing up in Texas, will always be connected to her homeland and her family there. The children in Kirabo Seeds will grow to be adults and will spread their knowledge of Jesus Christ and farming to their extended families and the next generation. Tonya says, "Life is so precious. My joy comes from providing hope for so many little ones."

Turning to You

You may not be able to create a home for sixteen children, but you may be able to donate to Kirabo Seeds to help in this ministry. Contact Tonya at *www.tonyalatorre.wordpress.com*. You may also shop their online store at *www.kiraboseeds.storenvy.com*.

Prayer

Lord, thank You for the joy that comes from being faithful to You. It is the only way we can know joy, for You state in John 15:9–12, "As the Father has loved me, so have I loved you. Now remain in my love. If you obey my commands, you will remain in my love, just as I have obeyed my Father's commands and remain in his love. I have told you this so that my joy may be in you and that your joy may be complete. My command is this: Love each other as I have loved you." Amen.

24

Love Heals, Understanding Gives Worth

Giorgia McPherson

Giorgia saw snapshots in her head, but she didn't understand them. She saw a brother and a sister whom she knew nothing about. She saw herself as she walked down a road, heard a noise, and then couldn't wake her parents. Let's follow Giorgia as she grows up and eventually gains some understanding of what happened to her.

Rich and Ann McPherson went to the adoption agency. They had three little boys. Their youngest child had kidney problems, and they knew that someday he would probably need to receive a donor kidney. The child's mother, Ann, was the most logical choice to be a match and donate a kidney to him. The agency seemed to be the only way that they could add another child to their family. They were very interested in having a little girl.

There were few babies available for adoption in the early 1970s. Many young mothers were keeping their babies and raising their children by themselves rather than putting them up for adoption.

The culture in the United States had changed. Some of the stigma toward single mothers had been dropped by more and more of the general population. Black Americans and Native Americans began to look at the way white people raised their children. Many black families and Indian families decided they wanted black children to be raised by black parents and Indian children to be raised by Indian families. This stopped many babies from being available for adoption by white people like the McPhersons. Abortions were being performed around the country because of the *Roe v. Wade* decision at the Supreme Court level that made abortion legal for the first time in the United States. The babies aborted were no longer alive to be adopted.

The McPhersons had no race preference. Consequently, Rich and Ann turned to Holt International and their children's services department to see if there was a little girl in Korea they could adopt. They had been turned down in their search for a baby girl in the United States because they already had three children. Holt International started its mission in Korea and has provided adoption services to find families for children for over five decades. Holt International gave the McPhersons hope that their dream of completing their family with a little girl was a possibility.

It wasn't until the 1980s that Korea came on as a strong economic nation. Before that time, there was a lot of lawlessness and tribal warfare in various areas of the country. It is not clear what happened to Giorgia before her grandfather dropped her off at the orphanage at one and a half years of age. Most adoption processes were kept secret at the time. Rich and Ann were told that Giorgia's parents had died around 1972. Holt International kept all the records because Nebraska was a closed state. This meant that when a family adopted a baby, the communication between the birth parents and the adopted child were closed until the child reached the age of twenty-five. It was believed at the time that this was best for the child and the mother.

The McPhersons were delighted that there was a baby girl in Korea who needed parents, and they started the paperwork, going back and forth to Holt International. Without warning, the agency put Giorgia on a plane that had an extra seat and sent her to America. She arrived in Kansas City without diapers or a change of clothes at the tender age of two. When Rich and Ann got the message that she was coming, they were in New Orleans, Louisiana. They made a quick change of plans and headed to Kansas City, Kansas.

Just like that, they had a baby girl. Ann was so excited. She dressed Giorgia in pretty dresses, almost princess style. People would come up to them on the street and say, "She is so pretty. I want one of those." Ann always felt like these people were talking as if her baby girl was a dog on a leash." Many people said they knew that if they saw a new outfit in a magazine, they might see it on Giorgia before long. Giorgia kept hearing from family and friends that she was the luckiest girl in the world. The adoption happened fast, without proper preparation or knowledge of Giorgia's background. Giorgia was expected to adjust to a new country, new parents, and a new language immediately. No one knew about the frightening day on the road in her past.

Rich and Ann treated her as they had their other children. There were no psychiatrists to tell them how to help little Giorgia adjust. All the adults the little girl had known in her short life had disappeared, and her trust in those around her was broken. Now she was a princess without ever knowing why. It was not because of anything she herself had done. She followed the patterns of an orphan, as she always cleaned up her plate and wiped off the table—even at barely three years of age. She hoarded food and other items she wanted. She was given a yellow bathing suit by an aunt. Ann could not find the suit after their newly installed swimming pool was ready to use. A plumber found it three days later when the sewer clogged. Giorgia had thrown it in the toilet. She also was used to sleeping with other children, and she hated sleeping alone as the McPherson children did.

Some people told Rich and Ann that Giorgia was mentally retarded because of some of her strange actions. Ann discounted this because at age three, Giorgia had carefully unwrapped and rewrapped Christmas presents so that no one noticed. With four children and many packages, Ann had color-coded each child's packages. Giorgia unwrapped some of the packages, took what she wanted from the other children's gifts, and put them in her packages with her color of paper. She then proceeded to rewrap the boys' gifts too. No one realized what had happened until Giorgia got a G.I. Joe doll and several boys toys. There were some toys that wouldn't fit into the rewrapped packages, and the McPhersons found them in various places throughout the house.

Giorgia grew up and proceeded to go to high school. In her senior year, she had a breakdown. She had always been a good child, but all of a sudden she seemed out of control. She never did anything bad, illegal, or immoral; she was just hard to control. She brought strange characters into the McPherson's home and would not follow the rules as she always had. Finally, she had to go to a hospital for help. Much advancement in mental health had taken place by this time, and Giorgia saw some professionals. She told her story about walking down a road and not being able to wake her parents. It is suspected that, because of the area of Korea in which she was found, her parents had been shot down, and she and her two siblings had been left to fend for themselves. No one knows how long they waited before they were picked up by someone. At the hospital, Giorgia was diagnosed with Post Traumatic Stress Syndrome.

When Rich and Ann visited Giorgia at the hospital, Giorgia would just sit there, crying. Then she would open her eyes and answer a few questions. A few days later, Giorgia came out of her trance. The doctors were dumbfounded by Giorgia's clear memory of an incident that occurred when she was only about a year and a half old. Studies had proven, however, that this was possible. One lady friend of Ann's said that she was able to remember her parents' deaths in a car accident that occurred when she was only nineteen months old.

Giorgia's preverbal memories, changes in parental figures when she was very young, and adjusting to a completely different culture could definitely have caused her breakdown years later. Today, much more assistance would be given to a child and its adoptive parents. With the system today, Giorgia might not have lost her self-confidence and had the breakdown.

Giorgia returned home after a couple of months of hospital care. She proceeded to graduate from high school and then attended college for a year and a half. When Giorgia was twenty-four years old, Ann helped her retrieve her papers from the adoption agency. Getting the papers was not easy. Remember that Nebraska was a closed state. Ann repeatedly tried to get the agents to understand that no one would be upset if the agency turned everything over to the McPhersons. Giorgia's birth parents had been dead for twenty-two years, so there was no one to be hurt by the release of the papers. Ann also informed the agency that the material might help Giorgia know where she'd come from and heal her from her Post Traumatic Stress Syndrome.

The agency finally mailed Giorgia's records to Rich and Ann. Ann saw Giorgia's relief, through words and expression, when Giorgia saw her birth certificate. Giorgia said, "I really do exist." Rich and Ann had had a birth certificate made up for Giorgia when the adoption was completed, and the date of birth was the same as the original certificate. Giorgia was pleased with all the information, and now she knows that it was her birth mother's father who took her to the orphanage. Giorgia understood that this grandfather must have been overwhelmed by the situation that had killed his child and left him with this small girl. The love shown to Giorgia by Ann in this process, along with the information received, has eased many of Giorgia's mental concerns about her history.

Today, Giorgia is the mother of three children. Her life changed when she had her first little girl. Giorgia is a natural mother. This first child is now at a university and plans to graduate with a science degree. Giorgia's younger daughter is also gifted. Giorgia supports and cares for her husband, who has high-functioning Asperger's syndrome. Her son needs continual care for another type of autism. Giorgia is capable of dealing with all members of her family, regardless of their needs. She has come a long way from that Korean road and the horror of the snapshots in her brain. Her adoptive parents' love has been with her and helped her heal. They love Giorgia's children and are steadfast, helpful, and loving grandparents.

Turning to You

Giorgia's adoptive parents showed great patience when she was little and in new surroundings. They continued to support her when she had her breakdown because they loved her and knew that Jesus cares about little children. Giorgia's parents are with her now as she raises her family. "Then he [Jesus] said to them, 'Whoever welcomes this little child in my name welcomes me; and whoever welcomes me welcomes the one who sent me. For he who is least among you all—he is the greatest'" (Luke 9:48). "The LORD is good, a refuge in times of trouble. He cares for those who trust in him" (Nahum 1:7). The Lord was with Giorgia and her family.

Prayer

Dear Lord, please help all the parents who are adopting or taking on children who need homes. We know You love the little children. "You mark us with blessing, O God. Earth's four corners—honor him!" (Psalm 67:7 MSG). Amen!

25

Love Provided to Blended Family

Pastor Andrew Ragatz

Andrew and his first wife wanted children, but it never worked out. They realized that in order to have babies they would have to adopt. Luckily for them, this was over forty years ago. *Roe v. Wade* had not happened yet, and abortion was illegal. The possibility of getting a baby was real.

They applied to be adoptive parents, and the doctor in their town gave them a call that thrilled them. "You are the parents of a baby boy," he said. "Come on down to the hospital and view him in the nursery." Then they took Robert home.

Shelly was born naturally to the couple eighteen months later. The couple always explained to Robert that he hadn't been expected like Shelly was during her mother's pregnancy; being adopted, he had been *chosen*. This always brought a smile from Bobby, as Robert came to be called.

While Andrew and his first wife were raising Bobby and Shelly, a lady named Elaine, unknown to them at the time, lived in Seattle and worked at Operation Baby Lift. She saw a number of children coming to the United States out of Vietnam. Kelly was a misfit, as she was blind in one eye. Elaine loved her from the time she arrived in Seattle, so she adopted her. It wasn't easy, but Elaine took Kelly's handicap in stride and taught her how to crawl. No one had spent the time with her before.

Andrew's first marriage came to an end, but Bobby and Shelly had had the opportunity to be with both parents during the years that they were growing up. Their "blended" family became even more so, as Andrew met Elaine and they were married. This brought Kelly into the family with Bobby and Shelly. The two adopted children were loved, and they knew they had been chosen. However, to make things even more interesting, Elaine and her first husband had also adopted a son, Juan, who was three years younger than Kelly. He had come from an orphanage in the Philippines and had been placed on the adoptable role because his father was in prison.

Kelly was always thankful, and she became a remarkable woman and citizen. She is the hostess in a restaurant in Seattle, Washington. Andrew had told Bobby that he would help him find his mother when he was eighteen years old, but Bobby has never felt the need, as he has always felt that he had a family of his own already.

Juan is another story. Though he was chosen and loved by his adoptive family, he chose not to fit in. As a sophomore in high school, he didn't show up at wrestling practice many times. The coach didn't call Juan's parents because he thought Juan was just grounded again. Juan was a charmer, as handsome as any model, but you could not trust him. In the end, he became a ward of the court.

As Bobby grew, he was diagnosed with Marfan syndrome, which affects the body's connective tissue. This syndrome had been connected to unusual height. When grown, Bobby was six feet seven inches tall. He had difficulty in school and had some behavioral issues, so he was sent to military school, from which he later graduated. He entered Hastings College but made a mistake with drugs and dropped out. Andrew was sleeping one day when Bobby came by. Elaine asked him to wait a minute while she woke Andrew, but Bobby left, and they haven't seen him since.

Shelly is now a federal probation officer, and Jack is a computer guru at a large food processing company. And who is Jack? Jack is another biological child, younger than all the others. Andrew states that each child was wanted and loved and brought into their family. In two of Andrew's adoptions, genetics caused problems as the children grew. Andrew feels that these problems trumped the environment that he and his wife provided for them at the time.

Juan had ADHD (Attention Deficit Hyperactive Disorder), which made him oppositional and defiant at an early age. When he was little, he would turn on the gas of the stove top. His parents told him not to do this because it was dangerous, but then he would leave the room and turn it on again later. They had to physically stop him, or he would have continued doing it.

According to my research, ADHD is a real disorder. It isn't caused by bad parenting, bad teachers, or anything a child has done. The exact origin of ADHD is unknown, but researchers think the disorder may be caused by one or more factors. ADHD could be an imbalance of two chemical messengers, or neurotransmitters, in the brain. ADHD tends to run in families. However, this does not mean that all children in a family will have the disorder.

Andrew has noticed that children react differently to their circumstances as they grow. Some react positively to love, while others don't. Some children have problems, whether the family is wealthy or poor. Some have problems, whether they are adopted or naturally born into the family. As Andrew and his second wife dealt with divorce and children, they always allowed the parent, rather than the stepparent, to discipline the misbehaving child. The stepparent in each case was a welcome friend to discuss options for discipline.

Andrew's family parented all five children with the love of Christ and His offer of salvation, and provided for all the children's physical needs. When his daughters became adults, they told him that they had seen other parents who could be split on parenting because of divorce, but that this had not happened in their family. Each child had been given the home and tools to grow into responsible adults. But just as God gave Adam and Eve free will, each of us has been given the same.

Turning to You

You can choose to receive the love others give you and to acknowledge the God of your parents. You can find God as Solomon did. "And you, my son Solomon, acknowledge the God of your father, and serve him with wholehearted devotion and with a willing mind, for the LORD searches every heart and understands every motive behind the thoughts. If you seek him, he will be found by you; but if you forsake him, he will reject you forever" (1 Chronicles 28:9).

Prayer

Lord, help us to give love as Andrew Ragatz did. Also, teach us how to receive love and to know You and Your love. Amen.

26

Love Perseveres

Traci Yoder

Three times, Traci and her husband, Mike, went through the adoption process with three birth moms. One baby was stillborn, and two moms changed their minds. The third mother was only fourteen, and they walked through her pregnancy with her. Traci had a biological daughter who was four years old, but she and Mike wanted more children. They decided they would like to give their love to a newborn that needed a home, rather than go through an expensive medical process to have more natural children.

Emotionally, Traci and her husband were hurting. It seemed that all their work invested in the adoption pool was not providing them with more children. They had definitely been chosen by birth mothers, but they were not getting a baby. Traci believed that God had put it on her heart long ago to pursue adoption, even before she was not going to have more natural children. So they persevered in their quest.

A two-month-old child who had been in foster care came up for adoption. His mother had been given time to make the difficult adoption decision. Traci and her husband were delighted when they were able to pick up Isaac. This was the start of two to three years of constant doctor appointments and frightening times. Isaac had severe acid reflux. Foreign substances were getting into his lungs when he aspirated the reflux and the food given to him from bottle feedings, which caused respiratory infections. They fed him thickened liquids until the age of three. He also choked when the reflux came up after feedings, which sent more trouble to his lungs.

Traci had to monitor his respirations and oxygen level. He cried constantly and did not sleep more than two or three hours at a time until he was nine months old. Traci believes that he couldn't sleep because he was in pain from the reflux. He cried from the pain, and he woke up when he had difficulty breathing from the infections and from sensory processing issues he endured.

Not only did Isaac's health cause Traci fear and anxiety, but it was impossible to leave Isaac with others, which gave her little rest. They'd had to take out a loan to pay for the adoption, and medical expenses became outstanding balances. Tracy worried about how they would pay it all back. Her daughter and husband supported her during this time, as did Mike's workplace, which gave him an unexpected bonus that paid all the medical bills and adoption loan. Traci and Mike believe that God provided that bonus. "And my God will meet all your needs according to his glorious riches in Christ Jesus" (Philippians 4:19).

Isaac is now seven years old and is doing much better. He has some tendencies that occur with ADHD (attention deficit hyperactivity disorder), but he has never been diagnosed. There was no prenatal care and possibly some drug use when Isaac's birth mother was carrying him.

Traci felt that God was saying to her, "If you say you want women to choose life, then you need to be involved in helping women make that life decision." It resonated with Traci that she needed to actively care for children born to mothers who could not raise them. She realized that God was putting it on her heart to pursue another adoption. "Whether you turn to the right or to the left, your ears will hear a voice behind you, saying, 'This is the way; walk in it'" (Isaiah 30:21).

Traci and Mike started looking into international and domestic adoption. Mike's job changed, and they had to move from their home. Because of the housing market crash, they lost all of their accumulated value in the sale of their house. It was now financially scary for them to adopt, but they felt they could trust God, and they continued with a domestic adoption. They completed a home study and were legally ready to provide a home to another child.

While they were going through foster care training, they got a call from an agency that had their profile but no signed agreement. Soon they were chosen by a birth mom through this agency. They were very excited, but after they heard about the finances required, they began to wonder if they would be able to pay the full amount. Traci's daughter saw her mother praying for and sometimes talking about getting another child who needed a home. She told Traci, "Mom, if God tells you to do something, He will provide a way." With that encouragement, they jumped in, not knowing where the money would come from, but trusting in God's plan.

The problem of paying the birth mom's living expenses and attorney fees weighed heavily on this young family in their new city. Traci took almost all the money from their savings and was driving to the post office to pay the bills. Just then, she got a call on her cell phone informing her that they were going to receive money from an adoption fund. This relieved her and gave her confirmation to move forward. Traci says, "God took care of it all." "How gracious he will be when you cry for help! As soon as he hears, he will answer you" (Isaiah 30:19b).

A lady Traci met in her community Bible study said that the group would become fundraisers for the Yoders. In the end, the woman held two fundraising events, and Traci feels that she couldn't have completed the adoption without this lady's involvement.

During the birth mom's pregnancy, Traci and Mike talked to her and waited for the baby to be born. They had everything in place, their bags packed, and waited for a call. Unbelievably, though, the call that came was not what they were expecting. The birth mom had chosen to keep her baby, but another baby had been left at the hospital under the safe-haven law. This law allowed a person to leave a baby at the hospital, no questions asked. This baby was being discharged from the hospital and needed a home. A birth mom in some kind of trouble had left this newborn baby boy.

Because the Yoders had all the legal paperwork in place and their bags packed, they were able to pick up the newborn when he was just four days old. They called him Cody. Now they had a daughter and two boys. Traci says, "I love God's plan. He knew the exact timing of everything." "Delight yourself in the LORD and he will give you the desires of your heart" (Psalm 37:4). "There is a time for everything" (Ecclesiastes 3:1a).

God continued to provide financially for the Yoders. They had to spend two weeks in the state where Cody was born, waiting for clearance to take him across state lines. This added more expenses. Post-placement visits after returning home cost money too. When these payments came due, they got a call from their pastor that an anonymous donor had given the money to help with their adoption. Can you believe it? It was just enough to pay those bills.

After moving to a new city, Traci and Mike were amazed at how many people—even people they did not know—were part of God's plan for one little baby's life. Traci says, "God cares so deeply and loves each one of us so much!"

Turning to You

If you have a desire to foster or adopt young children, believe that God will help you find the funds. Traci and her husband desired to care for little ones, and God was with them and answered her prayers. "If I had cherished sin in my heart, the Lord would not have listened; but God has surely listened and heard my voice in prayer.

Praise be to God, who has not rejected my prayer or withheld his love from me!" (Psalm 66:18–20).

Prayer

"Search me, O God, and know my heart; test me and know my anxious thoughts. See if there is any offensive way in me, and lead me in the way everlasting" (Psalm 139:23–24). Amen.

The Great Size of an Adoptive Mother's Love

Deb Kilian

Even as a child, the thought of children without parents to love them permeated Deb Kilian's mind. She loved to play orphanage. She was too big to play with dolls, but she would line up her little sister's dolls and pretend that she had an orphanage. She wanted a large family, but she had heard about the idea of zero population growth, which was prevalent at the time and kept many young families from having that third or fourth child. This made her feel that she shouldn't have more than two children or she would be helping to overpopulate the earth. But she could adopt orphans. She was so interested in having lots of children that she even dreamed about having twins.

Before Deb married, she discussed the possibility of adoption with her fiancé, Gary. After having two children, Gary was transferred by the US Navy to Korea. They knew how much time and expense was involved in foreign adoption while living in America. Consequently, while they were in Korea, they wanted to proceed with adoptions there. Two days before Christmas, Gary brought home a two-week-old baby boy. Gary, not Deb, started their adoptions of many children. She took one look at the little baby and knew they could raise this baby in their family. They were able to process the paperwork quickly, and on their anniversary, Phillip joined their family. He was very close to the age of their second child, Allen, so Deb now had her "twins." Phillip had been left with a janitor at the city hall.

Deb loved the children, but she also had rules and disciplined them in kind ways. One day, Deb sent her oldest child, Kristen, to her room. Kristen was crying and wouldn't quit, even after Deb had provided everything she needed. Deb said to Kristen, "You can continue crying if you need to, but you will have to go to your room." As Kristen walked down the hallway to her room, she turned to Deb and said, "Mother, you are a hard lady." Gary and Deb had to laugh at the remarks that came from a two-year-old. They both loved these surprises that came from the mouths of little ones.

Gary worked as a medical doctor, and he had some duty at the orphanage in the city where they lived in Korea. The couple opened their home to another child, Michael, who was four and a half years old. Michael had been left at the orphanage by his uncle. There was very little information about Michael given to the orphanage. The Kilians had already decided to take children with disabilities, and Michael had been injured in a car/bicycle accident. His hip had been operated on, but there were continuing problems. They adopted him as they had Phillip, just two days before Christmas.

In 1976 they returned to the United States, and Gary became a resident at Camp Pendleton in California, which took most of Gary's waking hours. Deb was certainly busy with their four children. At times, though, she looked at her family and felt that someone was missing. She would pass those feelings off, not knowing what to think of them. She and Gary had buckled everyone into the car to head out to a park. He looked back and said to Deb, "Someone is missing." Deb looked and saw all four children. She was puzzled.

Remembering her own feelings about someone missing, she told Gary about it. They had both experienced this strange sensation, which caused them to search for another child. Maybe the Lord was telling them that there were other children who needed a family. Then Joshua entered their lives. He was blind and autistic.

In 1980 Gary and Deb went to social services and found a beautiful three-year-old girl named Dana. She was absolutely gorgeous. She also had anger problems, but they knew—or thought they knew—that they could care for her. They went through the adoption process again.

In 1983 the social services at Gary's work knew of his adoptions and asked if he would take Sharon. Sharon, who was eleven years old, had spent much of her life in a Shriners type of hospital in New Mexico because of spina bifida and mild retardation. Among hospitals and foster homes, she had been bounced around a lot. Gary and Deb adopted again.

One month after Sharon came to be part of their family, Deb realized that she was pregnant with their daughter Sarah. When Sarah was about five years old, another physically disabled girl joined the family because of another request by social services. Tatiana—or Tati, as they called her—was fifteen months old.

In 1992 the family moved to Nebraska. A lady from Holt International contacted the Kilians and asked if they would take HaNa. Gary and Deb felt that they had their hands full and said no for the first time. The commitments they had already made were heavy, and they now realized the tremendous responsibility of raising children who were emotionally hurt. HaNa had been placed in an adoption situation in California for five years, but the family had returned her to the adoption agency. Deb said, "Hmm, I never tried that myself." She knew she could never hurt a child by rejecting it. So, when Holt called again and asked them to take HaNa, they accepted her into their family, adopting their seventh child. They now had ten children.

Four years later, the Holt agency called again. Their eighth adoption went through, and they provided a home for an eight-year-old boy who needed emergency placement. Nathaniel, who said, "I don't want to be Nathaniel; I want to be Daniel," was placed in their home. He had been abused by his own father, so the Kilians agreed to change his name to Daniel. They added Manahar as his middle name at his request. Manahar means "very attractive," and they all agreed to the addition.

With much prayer, patience, and love, Gary and Deb raised their eleven children. Deb knows that many children who are not perfect are aborted today. Although she had many struggles, she knows that each child is a child of God and that each one's life has worth. She has learned much from them. Deb knows the purpose of her life. She is a faithful person who serves our Father in heaven. Like all of us who have raised children, Deb understands that she wasn't a perfect mother, but she tried to follow our Lord's teachings as much as humanly possible.

Following are some of the difficulties Deb was dealt in her journey, described as if each child was a boy.

One of the adopted children screamed for up to forty minutes, five to seven times a day. He never lost the anger, hostility, and manipulativeness he possessed when he arrived at the Kilian household. This child wanted to hurt Deb. At ten years of age, he came flying at Deb. Deb responded by saying, "I am not the one who hurt you." The child said, "I know that, but I am going to hurt you for the rest of your life." One time, Deb called Gary to come home and help, but upon hearing her make the call, the child behaved a little better. Three hospitalizations didn't help, and the Kilians finally looked for a facility to care for this child.

One child would stay on the floor for hours with his hands on his eyeballs. He especially liked the warmth of sunshine. He would walk around the top of the dining table like a small child. Deb tried to stop him, but it was something he always did. The child never fell off the table, in spite of her worries.

Another adopted child kept hitting his head and always had bruises. They arrived at the park one day, and Deb heard that her child had been hitting himself in the head in the car. This was normal for him, but when she checked on him, he was black and blue and bleeding. Deb tried putting socks on his hands and wrapping foam rubber around them, and then she held him close to her. She ended up holding the child in a rocking chair for hours. Deb learned to hold this wiry child while doing everything else with one hand. This made her job as a mother and homemaker much more difficult, and finally they had to have him institutionalized. He needed constant attention because his tendency was to explore everything orally, and he was a danger to himself. When he was eight years old, the authorities in Albuquerque, New Mexico, decided that he needed to be in school. He was sent to the Alamogardo School in New Mexico. Deb learned that the child did not miss his family while at the school, but he did return to their home for summers and holidays. His world did not exist beyond the arm's reach. At age twelve, this child became an unmanageable adolescent.

One of their adopted children passed away from natural causes in 2009.

It took two years for one child to be able to verbalize memories of his past. He would ask for water and say thank you, but it was six months before he communicated further with the family. Only arm and leg actions in a fighting motion expressed some feelings.

Another child had severe medical needs. He had been born with an incomplete esophagus and had actually died twice but had been saved both times. He was fed with a food pump. After several surgeries, he was able to eat, but he was afraid to do so. After that, Deb worked out a game in which he eventually allowed crumbled Rice Krispies cereal to be placed on his lips. The child began to eat.

An eight-year-old had tantrums like a small child. This child had experienced horrible things from his father, who was a pedophile and predator. Being of marginal intelligence, this child will be under constant care forever. He is in a home for adults now and has no contact with anyone in the family except Gary and Deb.

Gary and Deb see one of their grown children in the Mosaic Home three or four times a year. They bring M&Ms and sit with him for ten or twenty minutes. The adult child then shoves them away, showing when he believes the visit should be over. A few minutes are enough now because Gary and Deb know they welcomed him as a child.

Children were special to Jesus. "People were bringing little children to Jesus to have him touch them, but the disciples rebuked them. When Jesus saw this, he was indignant. He said to them, 'Let the little children come to me, and do not hinder them, for the kingdom of God belongs to such as these. I tell you the truth, anyone who will not receive the kingdom of God like a little child will never enter it.' And he took the children in his arms, put his hands on them and blessed them" (Mark 10:13–16). Gary and Deb know that each of their children, adopted or not, is loved by Jesus.

The Kilian story is one of a strong couple of great faith who made a difference in the lives of the children placed in their care. Only God knows the extent to which their love has been appreciated and has changed the lives of the children they adopted and raised. Deb says that one of the most difficult children has been a success story. She suggests that birth parents and adoptive parents accept their own limits and look for help when the raising of a child becomes too much for the family.

Turning to You

"When God created man, he made him in the likeness of God" (Genesis 5:1). "You are all sons of God through faith in Christ Jesus, for all of you who were baptized into Christ have clothed yourselves with Christ" (Galatians 3:26). Gary and Deb Kilian took their faith in Christ to a high level when they adopted their children. They left the judgment of who should have life to God, and they cared for all the children who came to them. As they parented their children, they grew more Christlike and demonstrated some of the godly attributes identified by Richard Strauss in *The Joy of Knowing God*.

> We readily can see the relationship between goodness and some of God's other attributes. For example, when His goodness gives of itself unconditionally and sacrificially, it is love. When it shows favor to the guilty and underserved, it is grace. When it reaches out to relieve the miserable and distressed, it is mercy. When it shows patience toward those who deserve punishment, it is long-suffering. When it reveals to us the way things are, it is truth. When it bears the offense of our sin and absolves us of our guilt, it is forgiveness. When the Bible says that God is good, it is referring to all these qualities and more.

> What kind of loving parents would we be if we let our children do anything they pleased, such as put their hands in the fire, ride their tricycles on the freeway, or play superman on the roof of the house? [Deb was called a "hard lady" by her daughter.] The authorities would probably declare us to be unfit parents. Our love constrains us to discipline in order to insure the kind of behavior that will bring our children future happiness. And that is exactly what our loving heavenly Father does.

Prayer

Oh, Lord, help us not to judge. Help us to be strong like these parents and always look to You for guidance. Help us to do as You say. "Therefore, as God's chosen people, holy and dearly loved, clothe yourselves with compassion, kindness, humility, gentleness and patience. Bear with each other and forgive whatever grievances you may have against one another. Forgive as the Lord forgave you. And over all these virtues put on love, which binds them all together in perfect unity" (Colossians 3:12–14). Protect today any children in harm's way. We ask this in the name of Your Son, Jesus. Amen.

Reason 8

Love from Temporary, Foster, and Guardian Parents

28

Love Them as If They Were Our Own

Michael and Renee Johnson

Michael and Renee Johnson have two biological children, a son who is fifteen and a daughter who is fourteen. They would have had more children, but she never became pregnant again, and the fertility methods they tried did not end up in a pregnancy. They were thankful for their two children and proceeded to raise them, understanding that there would be no more.

After hearing about the need for more foster parents, and knowing that their son and daughter would be launched out into the world in only a few years, Michael and Renee contemplated serving children as foster parents. In the summer of 2012, they became licensed as foster parents. The requirements are not as easy as they used to be but the time spent in the classes prepares foster parents, enabling them to provide loving, stable homes immediately. Even though Renee was a stay-at-home mom with experience in raising two children, Michael and Renee were willing to spend time learning to be the best foster parents they could be. They even joined a foster parent group, giving more of their time to this service for children.

They were thankful for the preparation because it wasn't long before they had three brothers under the age of three years placed in their care. Imagine having two teenagers and then being bombarded with three young toddlers at once! Not only were the Johnsons cast into baby mode again, but the boys were not well. Remember those nights when you stayed up with a little one who had a fever, diarrhea, or a runny nose? In spite of the drastic change to their lifestyle, they cared for those little ones with a love that left them grieving when they lost the boys after a week and a half. They had settled into a rhythm and were beginning to believe that they could handle all three of them and keep the siblings together. When the boys went to live with a family member who had chosen to raise them, the boys were well, sleeping at night, and enjoying the Johnson home. It had to have been love pouring out to those little boys for Michael and Renee to have adjusted to them so quickly.

Another call came fairly quickly. The lady on the phone said, "We have a baby boy who needs a place to stay. You can pick him up tomorrow. He will be about twenty-four hours old when you come. This baby is being removed from the home because of charges filed against the parents. A sibling has already been removed because of abuse." Michael and Renee remembered the three little boys who had recently left their care. They realized that their hearts held enough love to welcome this tiny new boy into their home.

The Johnsons currently realize that the baby's case has not been decided yet. He could be removed at any time. They could go through the same heartache again. It doesn't matter to them. Their service is needed. This baby needs love, and they know they can love him as they did their own children. They are aware of the laws that allow for permanent placement outside of the parents' home, and the laws that return babies to their parents. They will follow the law. In the meantime, they will hold this child, sit up with him at night when needed, provide the food and clothes he needs, and believe that he might be theirs to raise to adulthood. This possibility gives them hope. No law will keep them from loving this child right now. They are just that kind of people.

Turning to You

The Johnsons are accepting foster children and giving them honor in their home. They show sincerity and brotherly love to each child brought to them. They want each child to be in a caring, safe home. "God's guidance is always guidance to love. Loving ways are the right paths (or paths of righteousness) that God desires to lead us on. Our sin is a result of our choosing to walk paths that are less than loving. We need God to heal and forgive our waywardness and to teach us and guide us in God's way of love" (from Psalm 23, *LifeGuide Bible Study*).

Advice often given to unmarried mothers in support of abortion is this: don't bring an unwanted baby into the world so that it will be abused. Parents interviewed for the stories in this book illustrate how much adoptive parents care for the little ones in their charge. The number of loving people waiting for babies is more than the number of babies waiting for loving homes. This statistic helps to assure that most children who are adopted are placed in homes where there is love. "All children are beautiful when they are loved," says Bertha "Grandma" Holt on the Holt International website.

Prayer

Lord, please let parents who cannot raise their children know that there are many who desire to care for them and give them a place of honor in their homes. Amen.

29

Showing Great Love

Christy Kennedy

This story will warm a cold night, open up your giving, and show you what God means by the phrase "being the aroma of Christ." It is a story truly orchestrated by God. Christy and her pastor husband, Alex, were forty-six and forty-seven years old and had three biological children when they were led to adopt. They felt the need to show that they believed in the sanctity of life. How could they be pro-life without doing anything about it?

The Kennedys contacted Arrow Child and Family Ministry, a state agency in Texas, and took a class, which took them nine months to finish because of their busy church schedule. Their home was inspected for safety and became a licensed foster care home. Life went on as usual, and Christy made a trip to Spain to see their twenty-one-year-old daughter, who was studying there.

Christy hadn't been home from Spain for long and was working out at their gym on a stationary bicycle, when her husband called and said that she had to get home because a baby was coming to their home. She got off the bike and returned home to learn that a Hispanic child, born in Houston, Texas, on October 30, 2009, needed a home immediately. Would they take this child? They had decided beforehand that they would take a girl, but this opportunity had come up rather quickly. Within twelve hours, they had a baby girl. It was November 3, 2009. The baby was brought to them by the Child Protective Services, which serves as a buffer to the Arrow Agency.

Keep in mind that, besides the child in Spain, the Kennedys had a nineteen-year-old at the university and a twelve-year-old still at home. All their baby things were gone. Christy's friends said, "Come on, we are going to BabiesRUs." Christy said, "Wait a minute, we don't have the funds to buy these new things." But her friends argued, "We are here to help."

The baby was tiny: only five pounds one ounce. She had the blackest hair. Even though Christy was ill prepared to have this baby so quickly, she realized that God must have prepared her heart for this child. She immediately felt a bond and a heart connection. Not only did Christy have this feeling, but so did everyone else in the household. The parents had already talked about such an event with their biological children and had received their blessing, but they were pleasantly surprised to see them all become attached to the baby so quickly. God was definitely at work.

Some people say they would love to adopt a child, but they aren't sure they could love the child the same as they would their own. The Kennedys were madly in love with little Lexi from the moment they saw her. Some foster parents say they have to hold back a little so their hearts aren't broken when the child is removed from the home. Christy was not able to give this beautiful child only part of what she had given her own kids. She had to give her total love.

The little girl grew, and when she was about five weeks old, her biological mother stated that she wanted the baby back. Lexi was one of seven children the mother had borne, and five of those children had had their relations with the parents terminated. Child Protective Services set up a monitored visit for the mother and Lexi. The foster parents were not supposed to be included in this visit so that the mother and baby could have time alone. Christy's heart felt the pain of separation immediately after the call. As a follower of Christ, she was conflicted because she wanted the best for the child and her mom.

On a very cold day in December, the Kennedys covered Lexi up with blankets and went to the Child Protective Services office. Before Alex and Christy could give Lexi to the worker, a lady came in and said, "Oh, is this my baby Cynthia?" She came over and asked to have the blankets removed in order to see the baby. The lady was very sweet and asked if Christy was a single mom. Christy shook her head no. She felt that she must agree to the lady's wishes, though she did not want to at all.

The birth mom wanted to put Lexi in the dress that she had brought for her. In the process, as Christy and Alex looked on, the mother saw Lexi's umbilical hernia. It was not healed and looked raw and protruding. The biological mother said, "What is wrong with her?," and backed away. Christy told her that the baby was not in pain and explained exactly what an umbilical hernia was. She said that it would probably go away or could later be surgically removed.

At this point, the worker called the mother and baby into another room for the monitored visit. Christy and Alex were so upset they couldn't sit there any longer. They left to find a cup of hot coffee as comfort against a day that was so cold—both literally and figuratively. When they returned, Christy and Alex saw that the concerned mom showed fear in her eyes—at the same time that she gave the child a look of love. Alex couldn't resist putting his arm around the woman, as he felt her pain too. It was the Christmas season, and all should have been joyous. At the end of the visit, the mother looked at Christy and, seeming to respond to Alex's kindness, said to them, "Take care of my baby." It was all too easy to say back to her, "We will."

Later, Alex said to Christy, "This will be the last time we will see her." Christy couldn't believe Alex, but they never did see the mother again, and the mother's parental rights were terminated in August 2010.

Of course, the process was not as easy as these words make it sound. They had to appear in court the required number of times, endure the monthly official visits assigned to foster parents, and wonder if any other obstructions would be put in their way before they could adopt this precious little one. Two scheduled visits were set up for the mother or other interested party to see the child, but no one ever showed. Alex had been right. Not only were the birth mom's rights terminated, but so were the unknown father's alleged rights. Ten months had passed with this little bundle of joy in their household, and she helped bond the family closer together.

Christy was glad she hadn't held back any love, and Lexi was thriving. She deserved it all. She was no different from the family's older biological children. There was, however, one more time for worry to creep in, and the Kennedys were thankful to know that the Lord was in control. There was a period of ninety days when any relative could appeal the court decision. No one did. On January 26, 2011, Lexi officially became their child through adoption. She was named Alexandria Hope Kennedy. She represented hope to them. Alex's given name is Alexander, and Alexandria seemed just perfect. She was now part of the Kennedy family. There was some talk about calling her Alexandria, but "Lexi" seemed just right. Alex and Christy had their little girl named Lexi.

Turning to You

Christy says, "Often the world sees what you are against but rarely what you are for." She and her husband wanted to show what they were for, through their adoption of Lexi. "For we are to God the aroma of Christ among those who are being saved and those who are perishing" (2 Corinthians 2:15). Christy and Alex believed this to be true, and they showed their love so well that their church exploded by having around thirty children adopted in a three-year span of time. Unbeknownst to Christy or her husband, an Arrow ministry worker was in their church on the day they have named "Orphan Sunday," when Alex preached a sermon especially for all the adoptive families. How awesome is this!

Prayer

Dear God, we pray today that more great people like Alex and Christy will join the world of foster parenting. Thank You for "Orphan Sunday" in their church. Help us all to know the joy of caring for Your children in this world. Amen.

30

Love Returned in Abundance

Connie and Jack Geist

As a child, Connie was saved by an older brother named Bob. She was twelve years old when she was badly burned through an unfortunate mistake on her part. A person should never put gasoline into a cookstove with corncobs over hot coals to get it started—because it could blow up. And it did.

Connie was screaming and running in circles as her arm burned, when Bob came. He took rugs, beat out the fire, and wrapped wet towels around Connie's arm and all her burns. They knew that he had saved the kitchen and possibly the house. The doctor said he had also saved Connie and that the burns could have been a lot worse. In those years, many people put homemade salve on burns. Some of these contained lard (pig fat), tallow (beef or mutton fat), or oil of some kind. This kind of remedy would not have stopped the skin on Connie's arm from burning. Bob's quick thinking and action saved his little sister.

Bob grew up, married Rachel, and had two girls. Connie grew up, married Jack, and had three boys. One month after their third son, John, was born, Bob called and said that their new baby was a girl. Connie was sad and a little jealous because she had wanted a little girl. In Nebraska in those days, no one knew the sex of a child until it was born. Connie loved her sons, but each time she'd been pregnant, she'd wished for a little girl. Her three brothers each had a girl.

In October of 1967, Rachel and Bob called and asked if Connie and Jack would agree to be named guardians for Carla, age five, and Christine, age three, in their will. Of course, Connie and Jack said yes. They had gotten to know Carla quite well over the past summer when she'd spent a week playing with and getting to know Connie and Jack's three boys, Jeffrey, Mark, and John. The children had spent most of their daylight hours playing together in Peter Pan Park behind the Geist house.

A few weeks later, Rachel called Connie and said, "Guess what! We are going to have another baby." Rachel was a little concerned about how she was going to handle another child. She felt that her hands were already full. Then, to Bob and Rachel's surprise, the doctor told them she was carrying twins.

Not long after that, Connie and Jack went to Amherst, Nebraska, to a funeral for a relative of theirs who was also named Bob. He was the brother of their sister-in-law Barb, and he was only thirty-nine years old. On the way back home, they thought about stopping to see Connie's brother Bob and his family in Grand Island, but they decided against it. They were tired and headed home. That day was January 30, 1968. Connie remembers the date exactly because later that night, before the ten o'clock news on channel thirteen (one of the two channels most of the area received), she and Jack received a call they will never forget.

Connie's brother Bob and his wife Rachel had been killed in an automobile accident on a road outside of Grand Island, Nebraska. They were going to play bridge with some country friends. A pickup had crossed the center line and hit Bob and Rachel's car head-on. Connie's parents had wanted them to know before the news came on the television. Connie's first question to her folks was, "Were Carla and Christine with them in the car?"

The girls were alive. They had been staying with a neighbor for the evening and were left there overnight. Another neighbor took the girls and brought them over to the family home the next day. The girls walked into the house and saw the family members. Carla saw everyone and asked, "Where are mom and dad?"

Connie took her into the solitude of the bedroom. They sat on the bed, and Connie told Carla that her mom and dad had gone to heaven. "You are trying to tell me they're dead," said Carla. Connie had to nod her head. The two of them sat on the bed and cried. They hugged for a long time. Christine was passed back and forth among the family, but she cried for Mommy when it was bedtime.

When Connie had asked about the girls, she'd had no idea if Bob and Rachel had followed through with their plan to name her and Jack as the girls' guardians. She had only been concerned about whether they had been in the car too and whether they were still alive. Connie had lost her brother, Bob, at the young age of thirty-nine. They were still mourning for Barb's brother, and now two more young family members were gone. What a strange situation it was that both brothers were named Bob, were thirty-nine, and died so close to each other.

The three Geist boys were at home. When Connie called to tell them that she and their dad were leaving Grand Island and coming home, ten-year-old Jeff, the oldest, asked, "What is going to happen to the girls?" Connie said that they were coming to live with them. Jeff replied, "I was hoping you would say that." All three boys were glad and welcomed the little girls into their family.

The decision as to where the girls were going to live wasn't completely final, however. The terms of the will were debated in court on February 6, 1968, Jack's birthday. Other family members would have liked to have taken the girls. Only two pages made up the last will and testament of Bob and Rachel. The very important information about Jack and Connie consenting to be guardians of Carla and Christine was included. When the attorney was asked if the decision was final after the debate, he said, "Those girls are where they need to be."

Connie called Stan Hart, the principal at Hartley School in Lincoln where they lived, and told him about the girls joining their family. She had worked with the PTA and knew him well. When Connie asked if Carla could join John in his kindergarten class, Stan understood the situation and agreed. John and Carla went to kindergarten together and continued all through elementary, junior high, and high school together.

The Geist home was a bustling place with five children running in and out of the house and playing in Peter Pan Park. One month went by quickly. Then Jack's cousin's fifteen-year-old daughter, Cathy, came to the neighborhood to live with her grandfather. She had been used to having family around her and soon spent most of her time with the five Geist kids. She turned out to be a huge help to Connie, but in all respects, the Geists now had six children to raise. Cathy actually called Jack's parents Grandma and Grandpa. What a change for Connie and Jack! Connie was returning the love she had received from her brother to his little girls. Years later, Cathy remained so close to the family that she was like an older sister, and she stayed with the five other children when Jack and Connie had to go out of town. Cathy graduated from Lincoln High School.

Carla had been in ballet classes, liked them, and was allowed to start taking classes again in Lincoln. Christine soon followed in her footsteps. The boys stayed busy playing football and basketball. At times, Mark and John would play "dress up" with the girls and run across the street to entertain Jack's folks. When Carla and Christine had ballet recitals, and Connie saw the little girls dancing, she realized that she had two little girls, which fulfilled her dream. She had never wanted to get them in the way she had. Tears rolled down her cheeks as she watched.

One day, Carla came running in from the park and accidentally called Connie "Mom." They both stopped and looked at each other. Carla politely asked Connie if it was okay for her to call her that. She said she didn't know what to call her anymore, and "Connie" or "Aunt Connie" didn't seem right. Connie told her that she could call her "Mom" if she wanted to, and she truly became Carla's mom. Not long after that, Christine started calling her "Mom" too. Carla asked if she would have to change her last name to Geist. She wanted to keep her real mom and dad's name. This was agreeable to Connie and Jack. Carla still uses her maiden name with her married name in her signature as an adult. The name was something that she could keep from the parents she'd lost.

At one point while raising the kids, a penny lady came up to Connie at the shopping center while Connie was busy getting candy for each child. The lady told Connie that her children were so cute and proceeded to ask their ages. Connie said, "Three, six, six, eight, and ten." "Oh," the lady said, "you have twins?" Connie answered, "No, they are a month apart," and she went on her way. She had been asked this question so many times that she didn't feel she had to explain the whole scenario every time she was asked.

Connie and Jack put together a family plan during the children's teenage years. They had two food booths at the Nebraska State Fair for seven years. The whole family worked at making and selling fish and chips, and tacos. Connie and Jack had acquired a liking for the British version, as they'd spent Jack's military years based in England. The plan provided work and something beneficial for all their six children to do in the late summer months.

Connie and Jack held guardianship of Carla and Christine until each of them reached the age of eighteen. Jack walked the girls down the aisle when they married. Connie helped them plan the weddings. It was a joy to raise the girls with their boys, and they never ceased to love them, even through some of those tough growing-up years. The Geist family members are always in touch with each other, and their reunions, when sons and daughters come home, are full of children of all ages and love shared in abundance.

Connie and Jack are very proud to say that all of the children graduated from high school and attended the University of Nebraska. They all care for their families and contribute to their community in many ways.

Turning to You

It doesn't matter how children are brought into your home, or at what age; they can still be a blessing to you. You will find that you receive much more back than you ever give. Consider a plan that creates work that your whole family can do together. This will bring you closer to each other. "Dear friends, let us love one another, for love comes from God. Everyone who loves has been born of God and knows God. Whoever does not love does not know God, because God is love" (1 John 4:7).

Prayer

Thank You, Lord, that little Carla realized that Connie and Jack were performing all the parenting necessary to be a mother and father to her and her sister. It is awesome that You opened her little heart to love Connie and Jack as parents. Carla and Christine learning to love a new set of parents made all the difference in the world to this family. Love comes from You, Lord. Help us to follow Your greatest commandment, repeated in 1 John 4:11: "Dear friends, since God so loved us, we also ought to love one another." Amen.

Reason 9

Responsible Choices Offer Life

31

One Human Saved by Love

Amanda Wingate Bellus

Amanda stated, "Luke feels like mine, in a way." Luke's mother, Brittany, is a friend of Amanda's. She continued, "It has been one of my best life experiences." This is from a young lady who was able to score thirty points in basketball in high school. She consistently rounded up neighbor children to form teams for ball games after school in her poor neighborhood. Now she is married and raising a son, Braeden, and a daughter, Kamryn, while working with nursing students at a hospital in Oregon. After being blessed with her own children, she still rates her experience as Brittany's friend as one of the best.

While the two friends were attending nursing school, Amanda found out that Brittany was four or five weeks pregnant. To make matters worse, Brittany was not dating the father anymore. Many night talks happened between the two friends. The young mother-to-be was struggling to stay in school, had no way to take care of a child in her dorm room, and felt completely confused. She was fighting the thought of options available to her, along with feeling nauseated from morning sickness.

The two young women met again, just the two of them. They hadn't told anyone else about Brittany's pregnancy. Brittany confided in Amanda and told her she had a date for an abortion in ten days. Amanda's heart sank. Brittany continued, "This is the only way I can handle this at the present time. I can't have a baby. I would not have enough funds to care for it and continue school. My parents would be so angry and embarrassed. They have given up so much to put me here. My dream is to help other people. I have always wanted to be a nurse. It is the only way I can stay on the track I am on."

Amanda thought and thought, and she prayed. Ten days, she realized, was all she had to change her friend's mind. She needed wisdom and tact. She wanted her friend in later years to think about this time without regret. Could she really dispose of the life inside her and never look back? Amanda believed it would be impossible for Brittany to become a nurse after destroying a life, and then forget about it. She had grown to love her friend, and she wanted the best for her in all situations.

Matt, Amanda's husband, prayed with her and asked the Lord what they could do to help Brittany. Then Matt remembered Cindy. Cindy was a lady at their church who had had an abortion while in her twenties. They had heard that she was haunted by the experience now that she was older. She actually had a ministry to help girls in Brittany's situation.

As they were carpooling to school, Amanda asked Brittany to call Cindy at their church and gave her the phone number. A couple of days later, Amanda asked if she had called Cindy. "No," was the answer. Brittany spoke defiantly and glared at Amanda for even asking. Amanda looked down, but she wasn't silent. She was praying for God's help. She had to carefully wipe the tears that kept forming in her eyes as she prayed for her friend all the rest of the way to school.

Two days later, as the abortion date crept closer, Brittany asked Amanda if she still had Cindy's phone number. The moment was huge. Amanda felt heat surrounding her body, as she wanted to believe that something she'd said had made a difference. She felt as if her heart was beating out of her chest. She gave Brittany the number again and waited to hear from her. To Amanda's surprise, in answer to prayer, Brittany told the father of the baby inside her that she was carrying his child. The father was speechless and entered into the discussion with Amanda and Brittany.

The abortion never happened. Brittany graduated on schedule and is currently working in a nursing home in Oregon. Amanda and the baby's father were the coaches at Luke's birth. The birth changed everything; the couple became engaged. They married, and Luke is a strong, growing boy. Amanda and Matt are friends with Brittany and her husband, and Luke is a joy to all. Amanda will never forget the feeling of answered prayer in saving his little life. She knows now that another friend of Brittany had been coaxing her to abort the baby and get rid of the problem. Amanda's advice showed that she loved both Brittany and her baby. "Love your neighbor as yourself" (Luke 10:27c).

Turning to You

Amanda played an important part in helping her friend avoid the struggles some women have after an abortion. Carol Kent, the author of *When I Lay My Isaac Down*, received this response about abortion from a reader: "When I was sixteen I had an abortion. For the past twelve years I have been dragging around invisible chains of shame and guilt. I've asked for God's forgiveness, but I still feel like a murderer. Why don't I have enough faith to believe that I can really be set free from my wrong choices in the past?" Thank God that we have these words from the Bible, which we can believe are true: "If we confess our sins, he is faithful and just and will forgive us our sins and purify us from all unrighteousness" (1 John 1:9).

Prayer

Almighty Father, Creator of us all, please help us to give advice from Your Word. Thank You that this little boy was saved by Amanda's persistence. Amen.

Don't Hurt the Grandbaby I Love

Geraldine Waters

Olivia, Geraldine's daughter, heard from her absent father. He wanted her to come and live with him. Olivia was nineteen years old, and her father had money. He drove the best cars and had a beautiful home. Also, he had children who were her stepsiblings. Olivia wanted to get to know these brothers and sisters. They encourage her to come and live with them. Olivia approached her mother and said, "I want to go and be with my father and experience his life and get to know him."

Geraldine wasn't certain that this was what Olivia should do, but Olivia was nineteen and no longer a child, and she wanted to live with her father. Geraldine considered the situation and realized that she has no right to keep Olivia home. She explained to Olivia that the scholarship she had worked so hard to obtain would be gone if she didn't use it now. But nothing changed her daughter's mind. Arrangements were made for Olivia to travel to her father's home.

Olivia arrived to open arms. Her stepsisters wanted her in their lives. Then the wild living began. It was a treat to have everything Olivia had ever wanted. Her father and siblings certainly knew how to live. It was awesome. She called home to tell Geraldine about the luxurious furniture, eating in beautiful restaurants, and the many gifts of clothing she was receiving.

Then one day, Olivia was expected to go out with a man she didn't know. Olivia consented and had a great time for the first part of the evening. Then things took on a different flavor. She was as innocent as a much younger teenager, and she didn't know exactly how to handle this man. She said no, again and again. Yet she didn't want to disappoint her newly gained family. She returned to her father's house, ashamed and frightened. The family didn't understand how traumatized she was or how she felt. She called home to Geraldine.

Olivia stayed at her father's house for three months. She was sick to her stomach and told her siblings. They knew what to do. They told her they would take care of her problem. Somehow it became known to Olivia that she was pregnant. She called home again and told her mother. She was afraid of the response, but her mother understood and said to come home. "I love you," her mother said. "We will deal with it. Please don't hurt my grandbaby. We will deal with the problem in the way we have been taught. We will take responsibility and give the child a choice too. This child deserves the right to live."

Turning to You

Love like Geraldine had for her daughter and grandchild is hard to find, but her plan was good. "Do not those who plot evil go astray? But those who plan what is good find love and faithfulness" (Proverbs 14:22). Geraldine wanted Olivia to stay away from impurity. "Having lost all sensitivity, they have given themselves over to sensuality so as to indulge in every kind of impurity, with a continual lust for more" (Ephesians 4:19).

Sandra Hilsabeck

Prayer

Dear Father in heaven, please be with this little baby as it matures and is born. Give Geraldine and Olivia wisdom to choose the best option for Olivia's baby. Let them know that if it is not possible for them to raise the child at this time, there are wonderful parents waiting to receive a baby. Guide them today. Amen.

33

Three Ladies Taught About Love

Terri Hout

Terri is now singing and telling her story, but this was not always true. We listened carefully as she told her story to The Women's Connection at the Hillcrest Country Club in Lincoln, Nebraska.

Terri's family was ordinary and included six children, five of them younger than Terri. They moved a lot because her dad was a hired hand and had to travel to where there was work. Moving all the time was hard for her, as she wasn't always accepted in a new school. She was used to moving, as that was all she had known, but everything changed when her mom and dad got divorced. Dad took her brothers, and the girls stayed with their mom. Years later, her mother met and married a man named Loren.

Terri was tickled to go to the University of Northern Iowa and get away from home. College suited Terri for a short time, and then she decided to join the army. This was during the Vietnam War. The United States Army sounded exciting and gave her opportunities she wouldn't otherwise have had while living in a small town.

Unfortunately, she decided to hang out with friends who introduced her to drugs. This behavior led to an unplanned pregnancy. She knew she could not return home. There was never a thought of giving birth to this child within her. The only guidance she received was the assurance that an abortion would cause a little depression that would soon pass. She decided to terminate the pregnancy.

Terri's life didn't change, and she found herself pregnant again. She got another abortion. After six years, she decided to leave the military and return to Iowa, where she lived with her sister and her sister's husband until she found a place to rent. She had no plans and no direction in her life. She admits today that she was a mess. Her profane speech was horrible (you know, the kind they bleep out on television during family time).

She got into an abusive relationship and tried hard to work things out, but soon she realized that the guy was just taking advantage of her, so she moved out. Then one day in April of 1974, she met three ladies. Marilyn, Heddie, and Lillian gave her a safe haven. They were different; their lives had consistency. They seemed to understand how to cope with her language and the rowdy songs she sang with her guitar. God gave the women a burden for Terri, and she attempted to love them back. She was not used to this kind of attention. Her stepfather, Loren, was verbally abusive, and he made it clear that she was not welcome at home. Her mom loved her but felt helpless under his control.

Terri started to genuinely care about the three ladies and responded to their love and kindness. This was new to her and was just what she needed. In their home, she felt safe, and she knew they cared. She did test them, however—probably for attention.

One evening after dinner in their home, Marilyn told Terri about Jesus Christ. It was November 1974. Not since childhood had she heard Christ's name associated with love. Marilyn told her that Christ had died for her. She thought, *I'm a failure. I couldn't stay in college. I've had relationships with guys, but there was no love. If I try*

Christianity, I'll fail at that too. But these ladies had demonstrated through their lives and outreach to Terri exactly what Marilyn was sharing about God. Terri thought there must be some truth in it. Terri longed for this kind of love.

Terri couldn't tell her new friends about the two babies she had aborted, because she was ashamed. But she did start to think about her babies more and more. Marilyn gave her a little book, which she stuck in her purse. Terri treasured the love and care of those three ladies, yet she was torn because she feared becoming a Christian and failing at it, just as she had failed at so many other things.

At the age of twenty-six, two weeks before Christmas in 1974, Terri was sitting at the kitchen table with drugs and alcohol in front of her—enough to end the torture of living. Something moved her to pull the booklet out of her purse. She remembered the day that Marilyn had given it to her. For a moment, she put aside her fear of failure and took out the little book. She opened the pages and read about salvation. Afterward, she prayed. She couldn't leave these three women who had loved her in spite of her lifestyle.

The next morning, Terri woke up, and something was different. She went to Target and bought a Bible. She raced home with her Bible and told the three women about her prayer. Lillian spoke up this time. She asked Terri, "Now, what did you pray?" After Terri told her that she had prayed to accept Jesus Christ as her Savior, Lillian gave her a devotional book titled *Day by Day*. Terri still has that book.

The three women had taken Terri to church with them a couple of times, but now, at the Christmas service, Terri cried and cried. They watched a baptism by immersion, meaning that the person was totally submerged in the water. Afterward, Terri said that she could never do that. It was too weird.

In January of 1975, Terri walked up front and was baptized by immersion as an outward demonstration of her new life in Christ. Her desires were changing. She even went to work at the insurance company where Marilyn also worked and felt comfortable enough to tell people that she had become a Christian and had been baptized. She invited her mom to church one Easter Sunday morning, and she accepted Christ into her life during the pastor's prayer.

Terri's singing talent came out, and she was making albums by the 1980s. Her Christian faith matured, and she joined Chuck Colson's Prison Fellowship Ministries by 1987 and became an area director for Iowa/South Dakota. She did her Christian work well and became well known in the area for her prison ministry. But she had never shared the story of her aborted babies. Privately, she told God that she would share any part of her life with others, but she begged Him, "Please don't ask me to share about my babies."

One January Terri was asked to sing at a Sanctity of Human Life service. As she practiced the song called "Bring That Child to Me" by Steven and Annie Chapman, something stirred deep within her. In the words of the song, a barren woman was pleading with a young woman who was about to have an abortion. As Terri practiced singing the words "the child you plan to throw away," she felt sick, as she realized that she had thrown her two babies away. She had been a Christian for thirteen years, and she was working in a ministry. She prayed, "Please, God, don't ask me to share about my babies." Then she thought, *What do I say to my babies when I see them in heaven?*

At the service, Terri sang the song and then confided in a friend who was involved in a pregnancy center. She asked, "How will I face them?" Her friend simply said, "Terri, tell Jesus to tell them how you feel."

Somehow, Terri drove home. Alone in her living room, she sobbed and sobbed. She asked Jesus to tell her babies how sorry she was and that if she had known then what she knew now, she would have given them life. Terri discovered that she had a mother's heart, even though she could no longer be a mother to her aborted babies. She grieved over their deaths by crying for weeks. Then, feeling Christ's forgiveness and finally forgiving herself, she gave herself a mother's ring for Mother's Day. It was a reminder that although she had denied them life, she would never deny their memory. It was also a powerful reminder that she was forgiven by God and by herself. She was now free to speak openly about her babies.

At another Sanctity of Life service with about four thousand in attendance, Terri shared her story of aborting her babies and her journey to forgiveness. She felt great relief in sharing openly about this secret that she had held on to for so many years. Terri turned out to be a great speaker. She was surprised at the people who came up to her with tears in their eyes after the speech. Some of them were men who had forced their girlfriends to have abortions. This experience helped Terri to become more open. She counseled with one young girl who was thinking about having an abortion so she wouldn't miss her prom. Terri encouraged her not to take the life inside her but to have the baby and place it for adoption. The girl did so. Terri also told her about abstinence, which would provide 100 percent birth control and would give her control over her life.

With a sigh, Terri said these words to the young girl: "If only I could have one day with my babies ... but I will never know them. If I had given birth and they had been adopted, then one day I might have known them. I robbed them of their lives, and one or two couples of the opportunity to adopt. It is one of my greatest regrets. They will never come to my door and ask if I am their mom."

Terri, no longer hiding her secret, became the first executive director of a new home for pregnant teens in Des Moines, Iowa. She was touched when she held the first baby born after she arrived there. The girls who came there didn't know where to turn. As a Christian, Terri was able to stand up for the babies' lives. She realized that if she had seen picketers or had been turned away when she went to abort her first child, she might have committed suicide. Here, she could save both mothers' and babies' lives. She told the pregnant teenagers to save their babies, and she gave them the tools for caring. She showed them how to make educated decisions about parenting and adoption. She loved the work and passed on her love—just as Marilyn, Heddie, and Lillian had.

Terri stayed with the home for pregnant teens for two and a half years. Then God had a new plan for her life. She needed to be available to care for her mom as she battled ovarian cancer. After they'd become Christians, she and her mom had drawn close to each other. Terri knew that her mom needed to come first at that time.

Terri was also led to apply to be a part-time nanny via a professional nanny service. Her song, "Bring That Child to Me" aptly described her physical ache to have a baby. She had numbed herself for so long, but God showed His forgiveness and put three babies into her arms to love. She became a nanny. She held baby Anna and cared for her about thirty hours a week for two years. Little Anna is nine now, and Terri still cares for her as needed. Anna and her parents are like family to Terri.

On February 14, 2009, Terri's newborn great-nephew Jackson was put into Terri's arms. Jackson is now in preschool, and Terri is caring for his baby sister, Kaylee Jo. She was changing diapers and loving it. Caring for these children and her mom have been the richest times of Terri's life.

Terri asks that we all take a stand against what is wrong. We need to give love and show Christ's love. Abortion providers need Christ. With Christ in their hearts, they will not be able to say that abortion doesn't matter in the long run—because it does. The baby's life and rights are terminated, and the mother is changed forever. Terri is sixty-five now, and she always thinks of her kids. Her life was turned around by God's love, given to her through the three ladies.

Turning to You

Find a Bible concordance and look at the many occurrences of the word *love* in the Bible. Here are a few that explain a little about the love we receive from God in spite of our sins. Every single verse of Psalm 136:1–26 states that God's love endures forever. Our sins are forgiven because of His love. "This is love: not that we loved God, but that he loved us and sent his Son as an atoning sacrifice for our sins. Dear friends, since God so loved us, we also ought to love one another" (1 John 4:10–11).

Prayer

Lord, help us to understand Your great love and to pass it on to others. Thank You for women like Terri who learned about Your love from three ladies and continues to spread it to thousands of people. Amen.

34

Pregnancy Takes Her to Loving Arms

Traci

Traci thought she was pregnant at age seventeen. Her parents had divorced when she was fifteen, and no one kept track of her. She told her older sister, who had married at nineteen, and her sister's husband about it. A girlfriend went with her to see if the test result was true. It was. Traci was pregnant. The only information she received was to get an abortion. She ran around with older kids, but she didn't seem to have anyone to talk to about her situation. Abortion seemed like a solution.

Traci went to college and became pregnant again. This time she ended up at a crisis pregnancy center, and this time the workers showed her what happened when an abortion occurred. The people at the center prayed with her. One person who was praying for her was so unusual that her prayer touched Traci's heart. A lady named Donna taught her about the Son of God, Jesus, who had died to save her. This led Traci to tell her parents about the baby and to rely on the words she had heard at the crisis pregnancy center.

Donna had told her that there were families who would allow her to stay in their homes while she carried her baby to full term. Staying with a family while pregnant sounded really good to her. She did not want to be responsible for another baby's life being ended. "Abortion is not the only option" were the words that kept ringing in Traci's head. Donna said that it was her decision of what to do about the baby, and no one else's. It was not her parents' or the father's decision. She was nineteen and was able to make the decision that would impact her life.

Donna helped Traci find a family to live with during her pregnancy, and Traci felt that it was the right thing to do. When she arrived at John and Penne's house, she was nervous. Penne reminded Traci that earlier in the year she had met her at a craft show she'd attended with her mom. Traci had purchased something at Penne's booth, and she remembered how kind Penne had been.

Traci states now, "John and Penne saved my life." She means this literally. They were the first couple she had seen living out their Christian faith in the home. Penne stayed up late at night, listening and talking to Traci about the issues of life, and sharing God's Word. Penne was always there for Traci. Traci's thoughts of running the car into a tree to end her life vanished.

The example of a Christian family did more than show Traci love; it showed her that God had a plan for her life. She hadn't been born to live without purpose. There was a reason she had been born, and God was always with her. This couple, John and Penne, had taken Traci in, just as she was, and had shown her unconditional love. This human love and the explanation of God's genuine interest in her and love to her—a pregnant, unmarried girl—were hard to believe. Traci was greatly touched by this new knowledge, and she remembers crying, crying, and crying. She prayed and asked God, if He was real, to show up in her life.

He answered that prayer. Here is a poem she found during that difficult time:

> Lord I am drowning in a sea of perplexity
> Waves of confusion crash over me
> Either quiet the waves or lift me above them
> It's too late to learn how to swim

—Ruth Harms Calkin

This time, Traci carried her baby daughter, whom she named Ashley, to full term, and Nebraska Children's Home helped her find a home for her daughter. The baby's adoptive parents named her Lindsay. Traci met Lindsay's parents in a counseling session along with Lindsay's biological father. During the first year, Traci received monthly letters with pictures of Lindsay. The communication was good.

Traci can now look back in time to see who she was at age twenty when the adoption became final. A very important desire of Traci's was that Lindsay be raised by a mother and a father. Traci could not provide that for her. It took a lot of prayer to go through the adoption process, but Traci knew what was best for her daughter. Penne was a friend to her at this difficult time, and to this day, Penne and Traci are friends.

It is never easy for Traci when Lindsay's birthday comes around and the memories of the little girl readily surface again. Traci knows her exact age and wonders what her daughter is doing. Traci realizes that her life was turned around because of her pregnancy.

After going through the program at the crisis pregnancy center for women who have had abortions, Traci volunteered at one of the centers in Florida, where she told her story. When others don't believe her, she shows pictures of Lindsay as proof. Traci tells them, "I'm no different from you or anyone else. I made a decision and gave my baby life. You can think you are solving one problem with abortion, but you are really starting multiple other problems. I had a really hard time when I realized what I had done to end my first pregnancy." Traci believes that she did the right thing in giving Lindsay life and finding parents for her. She left notice that if Lindsay ever wanted to meet her mom, Traci would be available and would always be thankful to Lindsay's adoptive parents.

Traci was able to graduate with a BS degree and move on to Florida State University for graduate school. Today, Traci works with kids who are behaviorally challenged. Many of them are depressed. They haven't made it successfully through any program. Traci's program is the last stop. She is able to say to them, "I don't care what you've done. You're staying here at school, and we are going to make things better." Traci knows that God is with her and always will be. "And surely I am with you always" (Matthew 28:20b). Because of this, she can be patient and never give up on a child. Recently she accompanied her fourth graders on a class trip out of town, and all of them had a good time. This work gives Traci a purpose for her life today. She passes on the love she received to the students.

Turning to You

Once we have accepted Jesus, as Traci did, and the Holy Spirit lives inside us, we have understanding. Paul talked about getting this understanding in Colossians 2:2–4: "My purpose is that they may be encouraged in heart and united in love, so that they may have the full riches of complete understanding, in order that they may know the mystery of God, namely, Christ, in whom are hidden all the treasures of wisdom and knowledge. I tell you this so that no one may deceive you by fine-sounding arguments."

Knowing Christ has changed Traci's perspective and her actions. These verses became real to Traci, and they apply to you also. You may not have discovered your purpose yet, but God has one for you.

Your life is important to God, and it might just involve proclaiming His name throughout the earth.

Prayer

Dear Father in heaven, please help us experience Your love, Your omnipresence, and Your purpose for our lives. Amen.

35

God's Love and Mercy

Lydia Percourt

Lydia was the youngest child in the family by quite a few years. At times she didn't like it at all; she wanted to be older. At other times, she was treated like a princess, unlike her older siblings. She wanted to have a relationship with them, but they had married and moved on. To some people, her existence was an accident, but others knew that the Lord had wanted her to have life. She presently works on many assignments in her church, helping youth and the entire congregation. Besides being faithful to her Lord, she is a great mother and wife.

Nothing could have changed the fact that Lydia wanted to grow up fast. None of the stuff of childhood pleased her. She started dating at age fifteen, and her choices of beaux were not what her parents wanted. She picked a bad boy, a handsome boy, who was quite different from her family. She was naïve, but he wasn't. He was experienced with girls, and at the ages of sixteen and seventeen, it was almost like a marriage. Lydia was grown up. She was sexually active.

Now, don't think for a moment that Lydia's parents approved of this. They had no idea what was going on. Lydia was very good at being hypocritical. She was Goody Two-shoes at school—involved in cheerleading, theater, and speech—and she was good at it too. Then there was the dark side of her life. Some of her friends suspected that she didn't have a normal teenage relationship with the bad boy. Lydia felt that some of them actually knew about her sexual activity.

The bad boy, let's call him Sam—was actually younger than Lydia, which probably was the reason that no one thought there was abuse in the relationship. This was not the case at all. It was a codependent relationship; he belittled her and told her she needed him. Looking back, Lydia believes that he needed her. Being older, Lydia graduated from high school first. She didn't take the freedom this afforded her and continued to let him manipulate and dictate her life. She portrayed one personal image of herself without him, which he wanted her to keep up, but he also wanted her to have the icky side with him.

At age nineteen or twenty, Lydia went to Planned Parenthood for birth control pills, since they didn't insist on telling her parents. There were close calls when she thought she was pregnant, but fortunately it turned out not to be the case. Although college was two hundred miles from home where Sam lived, she didn't join into college life. She remembers these as being the worst years of her life. She had moved from being prom queen, popular, and well-liked to being at a gigantic university where no one knew her. She had tried to get into a sorority with a friend but didn't make it in. When she received an invitation to her third choice of sorority, she decided not to join it. She later learned that her best friend as an adult was in that third-choice sorority. Joining it would have shrunk the campus and made it accessible to her. Having her boyfriend back home still calling the shots made her feel lost among the thousands of people around her.

The bad boy graduated and came to the same town where Lydia attended the university. He did not attend her school, and he soon showed that he had no goals to get ahead in life. Toward the end of Lydia's sophomore year at college, the relationship unraveled. She became aware that he was unfaithful to her. It was hard for her to believe, but people at home that summer said he had a crush on another girl. Having been sexually active made them emotionally connected, which was bad for Lydia. She felt very alone.

When her parents were moving her back to school in August of 1987, she realized that she didn't have any more birth control pills. She wasn't ready to stop seeing the boy altogether, so she lied to her parents and said she needed to go to the phone company, when she really wanted to go to Planned Parenthood. Her parents were glad to be with her, so her father got into the car and went along. There was no way to get the birth control pills that day.

Lydia went home for the weekend and listened again to Sam's story about loving her. Without the birth control pills, she got pregnant, though she didn't yet know it. Then someone told her that Sam had been messing around with a friend of hers. Her heart pounded as she called her friend to see if it was true. The friend admitted that she had gone out with Sam, but he had warned her not to tell Lydia. He said that if she did, he would trash her name, and she wouldn't be respected again. That did it. Lydia called the bad boy to break up with him. She told him, "I'm done. You screwed around."

Sam was devastated. He had his sister and his mom call Lydia. The sister said that they weren't married, so Lydia shouldn't be upset that he'd messed around. Lydia told her that they had been acting like they were married according to her brother's wishes.

On the way to classes, Lydia started feeling really sick. Her period was two weeks late. She bought an early pregnancy test. It showed that she was pregnant. She thought it must be wrong. This time she did make it to Planned Parenthood, and sure enough, they confirmed that she was pregnant. At that time, it was the late 1980s, and her parents were going through the farm crisis. Her dad was losing the farm. Her mom was going back to work. They still considered Lydia their princess. They had no idea about the dark side of her life. She couldn't tell her parents she was pregnant.

Lydia finally told her roommate, who called Sam and told him he needed to pay for an abortion. He came to her to say that he was sorry, that it had happened when he was drunk the weekend she was home. However, it was the roommate who took her to the city for the abortion. Lydia passed out before the procedure. It was ugly. It was kind of violent, like a vacuum. Emotionally, she just wanted the problem to be over with. She tried to pray and put it in God's hands, but she wasn't going to let herself hear anything different from her set plans. She believed that it was what God wanted at that time.

Finals week came. Sam's mother and sister called Lydia and said they knew that something had happened to her. They knew about the abortion. They said, "Don't let the abortion tear you and Sam apart." They continued to assure her that this mistake would soon be forgotten. Sam, however, was telling everyone he knew about the abortion. This was supposed to be a secret. No one was supposed to know about the bad side of her life. It seemed that her life was coming to an end. She continued to keep the secret, but when a friend or relative confronted her, she finally told the truth and admitted it.

Lydia's life was never the same. She lost her best friend in a plane crash in September. She proceeded through life like a robot. In March she met a man who was kind, generous, and openly Christian. But she had her ugly secret. She couldn't keep dating him without telling him. So she did. Then she said, "If you can't live with this, I understand." He was forgiving and accepting. She was surprised. She expected him to drop her. This was a different kind of man.

Lydia fell in love with this man, married him, and learned to love the Christ he loved. When they decided to have children, she had a very rough pregnancy, spending weeks in the hospital. She and her husband relied on their faith, and eventually she delivered healthy twin girls. Three years later, she was pregnant again and went in for an ultrasound. The doctor said the baby was horribly malformed and was going to die. She wasn't ready to carry this baby only to watch it die. She wanted the experience over. She had a D & C. (The medical term is *dilation and curettage* and is a scraping of the womb.) The baby was malformed and showed amniotic band syndrome, according to the geneticist. It had a beating heart.

Later, they had a healthy boy. Shortly after having this child, Lydia began to understand what she had done. The walls of self-reliance finally started to break down. She was in a Bible study when she came to the realization that these tissues she had chosen to abort had been children, just like her three living children. She now believed that she should have let God decide if their baby would live, not the doctor or herself. She realized that her earlier abortion had been a sin. Jesus died for the sake of sinners. Jesus had died because of her. Her babies had died because of her decisions.

She looked at her growing children and realized that there had been two more children inside her. She felt so blessed and thankful for her family because so many people would love to have even one baby. She believes that the baby she aborted after the birth of her twins would have died, but it should have been in God's timing, not hers. Since that time, she has heard of babies living, even when doctors have said they would not. She now believes that her first child would have provided a baby for some infertile couple.

Lydia is proud of her children and loves her husband. She goes forth into the future with hope and gladness because of God's merciful compassion and loving kindness for her. The Lord Himself described His character to Moses in Exodus 34:6–7a: "And he passed in front of Moses, proclaiming, 'The LORD, the LORD compassionate and gracious God, slow to anger, abounding in love and faithfulness, maintaining love to thousands, and forgiving wickedness, rebellion and sin.'" David declared in Psalm 86:5, "You are forgiving and good, O Lord, abounding in love to all who call to you." Lydia lives in grace because of the favor of love and forgiveness from our God in heaven, who gave His only Son to die for our sins.

Turning to You

Whatever you have in your past, if you turn to Christ, He will change you. "If anyone is in Christ, he is a new creation. The old has gone; the new has come! All this is from God, who reconciled us to himself through Christ and gave us the ministry of reconciliation: that God was reconciling the world to himself in Christ, not counting men's sins against them" (2 Corinthians 5:17–19a).

Prayer

Dear Lord, we thank You for forgiveness. "Vindicate me, O God, and plead my cause against an ungodly nation; rescue me from deceitful and wicked men. You are God my stronghold … Send forth your light and your truth, let them guide me; let them bring me to your holy mountain, to the place where you dwell. Then will I go to the altar of God, to God, my joy and my delight. I will praise you with the harp, O God, my God. Why are you downcast, O my soul? Why so disturbed within me? Put your hope in God for I will yet praise him, my Savior and my God" (Psalm 43:1–5). Amen.

Reason 10

Amazing Human Love

36

Mixed Adoptions Done with Love

Connie Jacobson

Larry and Connie Jacobson have four children, thirteen grandchildren, and six great-grandchildren. Steve, Bart, and Chadd Jacobson were born into the family, and their sister, Vicky, was adopted. Vicky and her two sisters (the older sister was named Marcia) were foster children in the family prior to Vicky's adoption by the family when she was thirteen. Vicky married early, and her first child with her husband was named Jodie.

Count the adoptions, and review the family tree. Think about the love you see. No one is left out. The Christmas photo has all of them in it. They are family. Seven were chosen, and eleven were born into the family, all before the six great-grandchildren were born. The mixture is so great that they rarely think about who was adopted and who wasn't.

Parents	Children	Grandchildren	Great-Grandchildren
		Jodie (natural)	Miles
			Marlee
	Vicky (adopted)	Shane (natural)	Zayden
		Rachel (natural)	Emma
		Erin (natural)	
Larry & Connie	Steve (natural)	Alyssa (natural)	Wyatt
		Danielle (natural)	Taylee
			Camden
	Bart (natural)	Ty (adopted)	
		Elizabeth (adopted)	
		Caleb (adopted)	
		Jessica (natural)	
		Joshua (natural)	
	Chadd (natural)	Sam (adopted)	
		Andrew (adopted)	
		Ella (adopted)	

When granddaughter Jodie was born, it was a little scary. Connie was only thirty-four years old and was not sure about being called Grandma. Larry and Connie had adopted Vicky when she was thirteen years old. They had been foster parents to Vicky and her two sisters.

Vicky called and said she was in labor on a day when Connie was going out of town. It was an easy decision for Connie to stay home and be available. The day turned out to be slow-moving, and Vicky needed a Caesarean section for the delivery. Vicky and her husband were nervous about these developments, so they called Connie to come to the hospital. Of course she went immediately and reassured the young parents that everything would go as planned.

It was a treat for Connie to see Vicky's husband calm down after she got there and to watch him being so proud of the baby after the birth. When Connie saw the little girl, Jodie, her heart expanded with the love that only a grandma can know. Holding Jodie was a precious experience that filled her heart with joy. She was instantly Grandma and proud of it! Soon she was called to Vicky's home to help with the little one while Vicky recovered from the surgery. This gave Connie a unique bonding time with this beautiful new granddaughter. This was her grandchild, no doubt about it.

Not having known exactly how she would feel about a new generation, Connie was now sure that the family was closer than ever. She was able to see Jodie's son Miles, her great-grandson, when he was only one day old, and the wonderful feelings she'd had with Jodie came back to her. Connie loves being with Vicky and her family, but distance between their homes keeps them on the phone, e-mailing and texting. Connie says, "With the adoption of Vicky, we added four grandchildren to our family, and we are blessed to be young enough to also enjoy the four great-grandchildren born through her four children." Connie enjoys talking on the phone with her grandchild Jodie as an adult. They cross the generation gap with their interests and catch up on each other's lives.

Larry and Connie's biological child, Chadd, and his wife, Kristine, adopted the first of their children, following Larry and Connie's example in the adoption of Chadd's sister, Vicky. Vicky's older sister, Marcia, who had also been a foster child in the Jacobson home, became a foster parent herself. A young teenager, Nicole, was placed in Marcia's home as a foster child when she was pregnant. Knowing that she was not prepared to raise a child and that she did not have the help needed to keep her baby, Nicole wanted the child adopted into a good home. Vicky mentioned to Nicole that her brother Chadd and his wife were cleared by the Nebraska Children's Home Society (NCHS) and wanted to adopt a baby. Nicole was blown away. Nicole knew that the Jacobson family had had Vicky and Marcia as foster children, and Marcia was now Nicole's foster mother. The situation was surprising to Nicole because she had also contacted NCHS. Now Nicole could meet Chad and Kristine and see if they would adopt her child. Nicole was exhilarated to have a connection to this couple, and they agreed to an open adoption of Nicole's son, Sam.

When the call came that Nicole was in labor, Chadd and Kristine were remodeling and painting an old farmhouse with family members Larry, Connie, Connie's sister, and a brother-in-law. Chadd and Kristine quickly abandoned the work for the others to finish. Then they had car trouble partway there and had to rent a car to continue on the way. They arrived just in time to see Samuel born, and Chadd was invited to cut the umbilical cord. How happy they were when the dark-haired little boy with the beautiful eyes truly became their child! It was a little late to ask, but Chadd asked Larry and Connie anyway: "Do you mind having a grandchild of mixed heritage to carry on our name?" "No," was the solid answer. Sam loved to be held, and he now had a large family that did a great job of that.

Andrew was born to parents who also chose Chadd and Kristine as his adoptive parents. On Monday of that week, Sam, who was four years old, told his parents at breakfast that they were going to get a baby that week. Kristine responded, "Only God knows when we will have another baby, so you need to pray about it." Sam came back a few minutes later with information that a baby would come on Thursday.

God does talk to children. On Thursday they received a call that Andrew had been born that day. "Jesus said, 'I praise you, Father, Lord of heaven and earth, because you have hidden these things from the wise and learned, and revealed them to little children. Yes, Father, for this was your good pleasure'" (Matthew 11:25–26). Imagine their surprise when four-year-old Sam was so right. God has a sense of humor and can choose what He reveals and to whom.

Andrew was not quite a year old when Nicole asked Chadd and Kristine to adopt a second child of hers. With Nicole's little girl being a half sister of their son Sam, they felt that it would be good to include her in their family. Ella has mixed heritage of black and white, and Sam is Hispanic and white.

After four adoptions in the family, Larry and Connie weren't surprised when Bart and Debra also adopted. They had two adoptions very quickly. Ty was two years old and in the foster system with another family before he came to their home. Elizabeth was a preemie born in Virginia. Both children joined the family the same weekend. Bart picked up Ty in Marshalltown, Iowa, and met Deb with Elizabeth (one month old) in Omaha as they arrived by plane from Virginia. Larry and Connie now had two more mixed-heritage grandchildren. Their sons told them they were trying to keep the families balanced. Ty is Hispanic and white, and Elizabeth is black and white. Connie was able to meet Bart and Deb in Omaha to welcome both children to the family.

Caleb was adopted in Nebraska by Bart and Debra. This adoption came about through knowing the mother of a teenager who was pregnant. There was never a question of accepting these children into the family. Larry and Connie included everyone they met. Being related by birth is not considered necessary at family gatherings. The more, the merrier! In fact, Bart and Debra didn't stop with the three adopted children. They added Jessica and Joshua, who were born into their family, giving them five children.

Larry and Connie consider each child a blessing and find joy in each of them, no matter what their heritage or race, but this does not mean that life is always smooth sailing. They have ups and downs, which they share, and the sharing binds them all together in love.

Turning to You

It is not easy to raise a family. The "downs" Connie talked about can be quite a struggle at times. They require patience and love. "Jesus replied: 'Love the Lord your God with all your heart and with all your soul and with all your mind.' This is the first and greatest commandment, and the second is like it: 'Love your neighbor as yourself'" (Matthew 22:37–39). The Jacobson family demonstrates acceptance of others, and there is plenty of love to go around in their family. This story proves the truth that different races can blend together in a family.

Prayer

It is Your will, Lord, that we live in peace with all races. Please bless the Jacobsons, who have joined three races together and called them family. Amen.

37

Adopting Love Affects Triad

Jennifer Crissman Ishler

Adoption always involves the adopted child, the adoptive parents, and the biological parents of the adopted. Jennifer Crissman Ishler, senior instructor at Pennsylvania State University, realized that this "triad" in our human race was so important that she started a course within the Human Development and Family Studies Department in the College of Health and Human Development.

Jennifer and her husband, Matt, adopted their daughter from Guatemala in 2005. This experience made the subject of adoption near and dear to her heart and caused her to research other universities, seeking classes specifically created for studying adoption. The only course she found was at the University of Massachusetts Amherst, which offers study on the psychology of adoption. Jennifer's research revealed a definite gap in this field. Raising her little girl gave her the desire to take this subject and develop a specialized course.

Some of the above information is from the 2012 Department of Human Development and Family Studies (HDFS) Penn State article entitled "Course Offers Insight into Complex Topics of Adoption." More quotes from government departments reveal the following:

- The US Department of Health and Human Services Administration for Children, Youth, and Families reported 51,000 domestic adoptions in 2010.
- The US Department of States Bureau of Consular Affairs reported 9,319 intercountry adoptions in 2011.

If you add four more people to each of the 60,319 people mentioned here, you have 301,595 individuals involved in the triad of these adoptions for just these two figures in 2010 and 2011. Some years show much higher figures. If you add all the grandmothers, grandfathers, aunts, and uncles to this figure, you begin to realize the enormous number of people affected by adoptions.

The course at Penn State revolves around the human emotions relevant to the entire triad of people involved in the adoption:

- Loss
- Sense of identity
- Rejection
- Guilt and shame
- Grief

Jennifer's reasons for studying adoption in our world today are compelling. She feels that we need to look beyond adopting small, healthy babies right here in the United States and look at the foster care system and international adoptions. She believes that the language of adoption is also very important. The words we use are important and powerful. For example, no mother "gives up" a baby. People "give up" smoking or bad habits but not children. Rather, it is more humane and powerful to say that the child is "placed" in a home. When talking about a home for a child, Jennifer's class extends to discussion concerning these three rights of every child: (1)

every child deserves a loving home, (2) no child should be without a family, and (3) none should be abandoned.

Forty-five spots filled the course developed by Jennifer at its opening. They enlarged the class and had to cut it off at ninety students. Topics covered were open and closed adoptions, domestic and international adoption, domestic partner issues, racial issues, and the positives and negatives that can occur throughout the adoption process. Crissman Ishler was quoted in the Penn State article: "Adoption impacts everyone. People are always connected to adoption in some way, whether they know someone who has been adopted or they were personally adopted. It's a great thing." Jennifer's class focuses on encouraging her students to think critically about the emotional aspects of adoption.

Turning to You

You have an identity with your family. You can be known as contentious and combative, well-known and loving, or quiet and barely noticed.

David said to Saul, "Who am I, and what is my family or my father's clan in Israel, that I should become the king's son-in-law?" (1 Samuel 18:18). "Sing to God, sing praise to his name, extol him who rides on the clouds—his name is the LORD—and rejoice before him, a father to the fatherless, a defender of widows, is God in his holy dwelling. God sets the lonely in families" (Psalm 68:4–6a).

Prayer

Dear Father in heaven, we learned from You in the beginning of the Bible that You created families. From the time we are born, we naturally have a desire and need for a family. Parents provide our care immediately. Teach us to appreciate the multitude of blessings a family gives each individual. Help us to promote this in our children. Thank You for giving us families, and help all the children who are alone in this world to find a loving family. Amen.

A Father's Love

Gregg Nicklas

After years of providing homes for children in Nebraska's foster care system under the name of Christian Heritage Children's Homes, Gregg and his wife, Lisa, came to the conclusion that they wanted to attack the reasons causing these children to need homes. Lisa felt strongly that they needed to start a fatherhood outreach program. Gregg and Lisa care that our culture has given dads the wrong message.

They contacted the National Fatherhood Institute (*www.Fatherhood.org*) and established a "Father of the Year" award for the state of Nebraska. Each year they hold a large Celebration of Fatherhood banquet. The finalists are inducted into the Nebraska Fatherhood Hall of Fame.

Their work with children and families is based on the belief that *every child deserves a family, and God has a family for every child*.

This is a brief history of their work:

- Founded Christian Heritage in June of 1980
- Became foster parents in December of 1980

- Opened a boys' home in rural Nebraska in September of 1981
- Opened a girls' home in rural Nebraska in January of 1984
- Launched a foster care program in 1987
- Started an emergency shelter in Beatrice in mid 1990s
- Opened two children's homes in Kearney in 1999 and 2000 respectively
- Purchased land in 2001 and started a neighborhood of children's homes just east of Lincoln, Nebraska
- Currently providing homes for over two hundred children daily, with the assistance of foster parents throughout Nebraska
- Launched *Destination ... Dad,*™ an innovative program that teaches parenting and relationship skills to incarcerated fathers and has reconnected over one thousand incarcerated dads with their children and families
- Launched *Family Finding* services to locate family members of children who have been languishing in Nebraska's foster care system.

They want to correct the myths that fathers hear and provide dads with truths.

Myths

- If you have failed as a father or have been estranged from your children for years, you should leave them alone and not contact them. They are better off without you.
- When dads are incarcerated, their families feel such shame that it's best for the children to sever their relationships with their fathers.
- There is nothing anyone can do to change your family situation.

- We don't know why kids have a bad feeling about themselves.
- Fathers are disposable. They are not needed in the family, and their children will do just fine growing up without them or spending years in the foster care system.

Truths

- Children want, need, and desire to have their dads involved in their lives, regardless of their age. Even if a dad has blown it, all children long to know and be known by their fathers. The fact is, children's lives will be more meaningful and fulfilling if their dads are actively involved in them.
- Fathers can learn to be responsible and involved parents while incarcerated. Change is possible. Your child has only one biological father and longs to know you. Christians meet with prisoners on a weekly basis. They teach the way of Jesus. "Come to me. Get away with me and you'll recover your life. I'll show you how to take a real rest. Walk with me and work with me—watch how I do it. Learn the unforced rhythms of grace. I won't lay anything heavy or ill-fitting on you. Keep company with me and you'll learn to live freely and lightly" (Matthew 11:28–30 MSG).
- Children who have a father at home are less likely to drop out of school, experiment with drugs or alcohol, become involved in gangs, become sexually active as teens, have mental health issues, commit a crime, or become involved in the juvenile justice system. "I long to see you so that I may impart to you some spiritual gift to make you strong—that is, that you and I may be mutually encouraged by each other's faith" (Romans 1:11–12).
- Dads can offset the bad feelings children have about themselves. Instead of using put-downs, name-calling, and

- negative comments, fathers can build up their children because of the natural respect the children have for them.
- A biological father can believe that he is saved as it states in the Bible: "Everyone who calls on the name of the Lord will be saved" (Romans 10:13). Because you can call to the Lord to be forgiven and saved, you will love your child, for "love comes from God" (1 John 4:7b). Therefore, a father can love in this way. "Love does not delight in evil but rejoices with the truth. It always protects, always trusts, always hopes, always perseveres" (1 Corinthians 13:6–7). A father with this kind of love is always needed in the child's home or life in some way.

Federal statute requires permanency for children. If a child has been placed out-of-home for fifteen of the last twenty-two months in the foster care system, the court can move for termination of parental rights to enable the child to be placed in a permanent adoptive home.

The Nicklases believe that children should be placed with their own families, if at all possible. They believe that *Family Finding* services should be available for all children who have lost contact with their families, that a search should be conducted to discover and engage family members in order to create a network of support and provide permanency for children in the foster care system.

Gregg and Lisa are motivated to find homes for every child in Nebraska. There aren't enough homes available. Gregg and Lisa tell father after father—at banquets, in prison, and wherever they can—how important fathers are to their children.

The vast majority of incarcerated men were raised without a father. Gregg and Lisa's work continues, and they ask all who can to join them. They are true disciples as they carry out Christ's interest in children rather than their own interests.

Turning to You

One story that shows how important it is for children to know their fathers and grandfathers is one about my own father. LaVern H. Johnson was born to a single mother. He saw his real father only once in his lifetime. When he was eighty-five, he convinced me to take him to Sweden to see the homeland of his single grandmother who had cared for him while his single mother worked to provide for the three of them.

As LaVern and I traveled in Sweden with the help of two friends, we found relatives descended from his grandmother's siblings. The joy LaVern received in learning that he had come from good people made him ecstatic. He said at the burial ground of his grandmother's siblings, "I come from good people." The illegitimacy of his birth and his mother's birth had kept him from that realization for eighty-five years.

The fact that his father had not been around to raise him and that his grandfather had not been around for his grandmother had affected this man greatly. This fact was not known before the trip to Sweden, because LaVern had prospered in his farming, loved his wife, and raised four children. Because he was a leader in the community, people thought that missing his father wasn't a big deal. The truth is that fathers are very important to every human being.

LaVern stood at the graves of his ancestors, which had Scripture written on the gravestones. Tears came to his eyes, and he asked the Lord right there to forgive him of his sins. He prayed to say that he wanted to accept Jesus into his heart.

LaVern had been taught the Scriptures, and now he believed that he had been adopted into God's family. He believed he was an heir of our Lord. "So you are no longer a slave, but a son; and since you are a son, God has made you also an heir" (Galatians 4:7). You too can succeed, because you can accept Jesus as your Savior as well. But never forget that our fathers here on earth are needed to show love as our heavenly Father does.

Sandra Hilsabeck

Prayer

Dear Father in heaven, please change our culture to bring about respect for fathers as Gregg and Lisa pursue this purpose. Put more fathers into their children's lives. Help more and more men to realize the difference they make in their own children's lives. Amen.

39

Adopted Because of Love for Others

Mike and Renee Holen

Mike tried to sign up as a soldier during the Vietnam War. Many young men from the rural areas of Nebraska followed their fathers' examples to serve their country. They wanted to ensure democracy and freedom worldwide, and they knew that their actions would help keep the United States a democracy with its power coming from the people. Mike did not pass the physical to join the military. But this did not stop him and his wife, Renee, from wanting to help, so they went through the Friends of Children of Vietnam and adopted Ben.

Mike and Renee believed that Ben was on the plane that had its doors opened, resulting in many babies falling to the rice paddies below in their cardboard boxes. This belief comes from the fact that baby Ben was shipped the day after the disaster. He spent four weeks in hospitals in San Francisco, California, and Denver, Colorado.

When Mike and Renee got the call that Ben was in Omaha, Nebraska, they dropped their two children off with relatives and headed out to pick up their little boy. Mike's sister, Mary Hamilton, received a call from the police in Loomis, Nebraska, that an adoption representative had already picked up the baby and taken him to Columbus, Nebraska. Without cell phones to relay the message, the Holens arrived in Omaha. The agency had three birth certificates and did not know which one was their child's real one. They were told to pick one of the three, as all were for a baby boy about one year old. They picked one with the name Tuan. They named him Benjamin Tuan.

As soon as they received the message that the little boy had already been picked up, they immediately headed to Columbus. Their little boy was waiting for them there—with scabies, ear infection, and diarrhea, and in need of immediate medical care. Ben was a one-year-old, full-blooded Vietnamese child with rotten teeth (caused by sugar cane sticks given to babies to keep them quiet), hair sticking up all over, and scabs and napalm burns on his head. It was amazing that in only a few months, Ben became healthy. His skin and hair looked great, and he ate until his plate was empty and there was no more food available. He adjusted.

Ben arrived in Nebraska in the spring of the year, and he was terribly frightened of thunder and lightning. Few here in America can relate to the sounds of war that permeated Ben's first year of life. His new parents held him tight and soothed him the best way they could, with a love for him that was growing every minute.

At first Mike and Renee had a hard time knowing what to feed him. He loved mashed potatoes, but they caused diarrhea. The doctor took junk out of his ears and told them that he would have a hearing loss. Later, Ben remembered the doctor who had hollered at him. They found out that he was lactose intolerant.

Eventually Ben adapted to life with his new parents and siblings, but this didn't stop him from biting someone who tried to take something from him. He even bit a journalist on the ankle while the journalist was trying to get Ben's story.

One day Ben looked at Mike and said, "Dada." Their hearts were warmed. Ben was adapting and starting to accept them as his parents. However, not everyone in the family was accepting of this little Vietnamese boy. Mike's father had fought the Japanese in World War II, and he had said to Mike and Renee, "Don't adopt this baby." Renee's dad wasn't interested in Ben either. He would hold the other kids and just look at Ben. When Ben finally said the word *grandpa*, Renee's dad's heart melted.

When Ben went to school, he was the only oriental child in the entire Loomis School. Ben was aware that his skin was different. When he was only two years old, he looked at a Mexican in the grocery store and saw the man's dark arm. Renee could see Ben staring and comparing his own arm to the man's arm. One day at school, the teacher was proceeding with a lesson to help the children realize the differences among children. The teacher told the child in front of Ben to turn around and tell what was different about the child behind him. The child thought for a while and finally said, "His shoes make different marks in the snow." The children in the school showed amazing acceptance of this child who looked different, and Ben became friends with many in his class.

While Ben was growing up, he didn't want to think of himself as oriental. He was accepted by the kids around him, and he acted as though he was Swedish, as most of the others were. In high school, he eventually visited with a young oriental girl. But after entering the University of Nebraska, his opportunities to mix with all races increased. Eventually he met a young Vietnamese girl named Maria while he was selling phones. Her dad had been in the Vietnamese military and had been imprisoned. Upon being released, he had taken with him what family he could—Maria, dressed all in black—and left his wife and his other little girl. He immigrated to Lincoln, Nebraska.

Maria and her dad were sponsored by a Lincoln couple in order to become legal citizens. Later, Maria's mother and little sister left Vietnam too, but three quarters of the people on the ship did not survive the trip, including Maria's little sister. Her mother lost several toes to the rats on the ship.

Ben became enamored of Maria and her story. They dated as they studied for their degrees, and eventually they wanted to get married. Ben had adjusted again to reality and his background.

Maria's dad and mother loved their new country, and they moved forward, having another daughter and son in the United States. Maria's father wanted her to marry a Vietnamese man, but he was very protective and questioned all her boyfriends. He decided to test Ben by asking him questions to find out about his character. The questions went like this: Would you like a beer? I have another pretty girl. Are you interested? When you go to the casino, which road do you take?

In this manner, Maria's father found out all about Ben. After Ben and Maria were engaged, Ben asked him, "What would have happened if I had answered the questions differently?" Maria's dad told him defiantly, "I would have thrown you out the door."

Having passed the tests, Ben and Maria married and are the happy parents of little Jacob. Because of Maria and the love of Mike and Renee's family, Ben is comfortable with who he is as an American citizen with a Vietnamese background.

Turning to You

"Who among the gods is like you, O LORD? Who is like you— majestic in holiness, awesome in glory, working wonders?" (Exodus 15:11). Oh, Lord, not only did You perform miracles so long ago, but You saved little Ben. You prepared a family for him. You saved his life and gave him the love of a ready-made family. I can only believe that You nudged Mike to want to help in some way. You opened up Renee's heart to accepting a Vietnamese baby boy from the baby flights of war. You softened the grandparents' hearts and brought Maria to Ben, who had struggled with his ethnicity.

"Give thanks to the LORD, for he is good: his love endures forever" (Psalm 107:1 MSG). "Come to me. Get away with me and you'll recover your life. I'll show you how to take a real rest. Walk with me and work with me—watch how I do it. Learn the unforced rhythms of grace. I won't lay anything heavy or ill-fitting on you. Keep company with me and you'll learn to live freely and lightly" (Matthew 11:28–30 MSG).

Prayer

Dear Father in heaven, let us believe. Let us understand that You are working miracles in front of our eyes today. Open our hearts to accept those You bring to us. Help us to follow the steps Mike and Renee have taken and follow You to help others. Amen.

Afterword

In interviewing sources, researching for this book, raising a family, providing a home for eleven foster children, and watching fourteen grandchildren, I have resolved to believe certain items to be true. First and foremost, I believe that God created humans in His image and told them to reproduce. "So God created man in his own image, in the image of God he created him; male and female he created them. God blessed them and said to them. 'Be fruitful and increase in number; fill the earth and subdue it'" (Genesis 1:27–28a). Second, we are told by Jesus to "love one another" (John 13:34b).

The above two commands lead me to believe the following statements. References for these ten statements can be found in the corresponding ten listings at the end of this section.

1. Abstinence (known today as *purity*) not only protects you from pregnancy before you are ready, but it saves you from being bonded to another person before marriage.
2. God placed into our bodies certain chemicals (dopamine, oxytocin, and vasopressin) that are activated by sex, causing a bond between a man and a woman.
3. The family is the basic foundation of human society. God provided sex as the glue, or soul, that strengthens, comforts, and brings children into the family.
4. Pregnant women are entrusted with the body of another person with a unique genetic makeup, independent brain

waves, and his or her own heartbeat, blood type, fingerprints, and facial expressions.
5. Women never forget the loss of a child that has been taken from them.
6. The baby of a rapist is not a mistake and does not deserve the death penalty because of the crime of the father.
7. A baby will not ruin your life. He or she will enhance your life. If you choose to provide the baby with a family through adoption, the adoptive parents' lives will be blessed. Many couples are waiting for a baby just like yours. They will love him or her and provide the stable family you cannot.
8. There is emotional and financial help for pregnant women provided by agencies.
9. There is an adoption option for every mother/father.
10. Societies that have promoted abortion find that they have aging populations without enough children, and uneven birth rates between boys and girls.

Turning to You

The Bible tells the truth about human reproduction. David proclaimed, "God created my inmost being; you knit me together in my mother's womb" (Psalm 139:13). The apostle Paul said, "Flee from sexual immorality. All other sins a man commits are outside his body, but he who sins sexually sins against his own body. Do you know that your body is a temple of the Holy Spirit, who is in you, whom you have received from God? You are not your own; you were bought at a price. Therefore honor God with your body" (1 Corinthians 6:18–20). "Turn from evil and do good; then you will dwell in the land forever. For the LORD loves the just and will not forsake his faithful ones" (Psalm 37:27–28). "The LORD helps them and delivers them; he delivers them from the wicked and saves them, because they take refuge in him" (Psalm 37:40).

Prayer

Dear Father in heaven, thank You for Your biblical truths. Help us to believe what David and Paul said about sins against our own bodies. Help us to be abstinent until we are married and to honor our bodies as the temple of the Holy Spirit. If we have not received the Holy Spirit, inspire us to repent of our sins and pray to follow Jesus. Provide an opportunity for us to be baptized and receive the Spirit within us. "Remember not the sins of my youth and my rebellious ways; according to your love remember me, for you are good, O LORD" (Psalm 25:7). In Jesus' name, amen.

References for the Ten Statements of Belief

Regarding the ten statements of belief earlier in this section, the following journals, books, and agencies will provide more information for you.

1. *www.WaitingTillMarriage.org*
2. *The American Family Association Journal* (October 2010).
3. Ramah International, *Her Choice to Heal Recovery Guide*.
4. Mark Mittelberg, *The Questions Christians Hope No One Will Ask*. Mark Mittelberg, "Interdependence: A Conversation Starter," *Acts & Facts* (October 2013).
5. Tina Zahn, *Why I Jumped*. Monica Lewinsky, *Monica's Story*.
6. *www.Pamstenzel.com*
7. Lincoln Crisis Pregnancy Center
   Daniel James Devine "Cynthia's choice, Meet one of the first women ever to undo her medical abortion" *WORLD* (May 4 2013)
8. Nebraska Children's Home Society
   American Center for Law and Justice

9. See the stories in this book (*Ready or Not: 10 Reasons to Love Your Baby*).
10. Jamie Dean "Double Jeopardy," *WORLD* (August 10, 2013). *www.OneNewsNow.com*, February 6, 2014.
    "Miracle," *WORLD* (August 11, 2012).
    "After decades of abortion, a pro-life detour ... in Russia": *www.OneNewsNow.com* (April 2, 2014).

Therefore, brothers, we have an obligation—but it is not to the sinful nature, to live according to it. For if you live according to the sinful nature, you will die, but if by the Spirit you put to death the misdeeds of the body, you will live, because those who are led by the Spirit of God are sons of God. For you did not receive a spirit that makes you a slave again to fear, but you received the Spirit of sonship. And by him we cry, "Abba." Father. The Spirit himself testifies with our spirit that we are God's children. Now if we are children, then we are heirs—heirs of God and co-heirs with Christ, if indeed we share in his sufferings in order that we may also share in his glory. (Romans 8:12–17)

We Are Called to Be God's People

Austrian hymn
Words by Thomas Jackson

We are called to be God's people
Showing by our lives his grace,
One in heart and one in spirit,
Sign of hope for all the race.
Let us show how he has changed us,
And remade us as his own.
Let us share our life together
As we shall around his throne.

We are called to be God's servants,
Working in his world today;
Taking his own task upon us,
All his sacred words obey,
Let us rise, then to his summons,
Dedicate to him our all,
That we may be faithful servants,
Quick to answer now his call.

We are called to be God's prophets,
Speaking for the truth and right,
Standing firm for godly justice,
Bringing evil things to light.
Let us seek the courage needed,
Our high calling to fulfill,
That the world may know
The blessing of the doing of God's will.

Sources

Calkin, Ruth Harms. "I Am Drowning in a Sea of Perplexity" (poem).
Condon, Guy, and David Hazard. *Father Aborted*. Wheaton, Illinois: Tyndale, 2001.
Fields, Don, Lifeguide Bible Study, Nehemiah, Lesson 7
Gillette, Carolyn Winfrey. "Long Ago, When Pharaoh's Daughter" (hymn). Bible references: Exodus 2:1–10; Matthew 18:1–5; Galatians 4:4–7; John 3:1–10; James 1:27; Psalm 68:5–6. Tune: "Come, Thou Fount of Every Blessing," John Wyeth's *Repository of Sacred Music*, 1813. Text: Copyright © 2009 by Carolyn Winfrey Gillette. All rights reserved.
Hastings, Patty, mother of adopted son.
Henslee, Julie, volunteer in Lincoln Crisis Pregnancy Center.
Holt, Grandma Bertha, Holt International website
Ishler, Jennifer Crissman, professor at Pennsylvania State University.
Kent, Carol. *When I Lay My Isaac Down*. Carol Stream, Illinois: NavPress, 2004.
LifeGuide Bible Studies, "The 23rd Psalm."
Mason, Mike. *The Gospel According to Job*. Phillipsburg, New Jersey: P & R Publishing Co., 2007.
McCarthy, Pat, director of the Lincoln Crisis Pregnancy Center of Nebraska.
Moore, Russell, dean of the School of Theology at Southern Baptist Theological Seminary.
Rosenblum, Gail. Article in *Star Tribune* (Minneapolis).

Strauss, Richard L. *The Joy of Knowing God*. Neptune, New Jersey: Loizeaux Brothers, 1984

Westphal, Joan, grandmother of adopted children.